I Still See Her Haunting Eyes

The Holocaust and a Hidden Child Named Aaron

By Aaron Elster &
Joy Erlichman Miller, Ph.D.

I Still See Her Haunting Eyes

ISBN 0-9759875-2-6
ISBN 13 978-0-9759875-2-0

BF Press
P.O. Box 3065
Peoria, IL 61612-3065
877-COPING-0 (877-267-4640)

Edited and designed by Monica Vest Wheeler

Authors' note: When G-d's name is written, it makes the document holy, and many Jewish people never write His name on anything other than on a holy document which will receive proper care.

Visit Aaron at www.aaronelster.com

Download Teacher's Guide at:
www.aaronelster.com/guide.html

Contact Aaron at: 847-567-0184

Book review

Aaron Elster's story is told with power and integrity. The memory is fresh, the experience searing. His work retains the tone of the child who lived this story, untainted by adult cynicism and uncensored by a desire to protect those of us who were not there or the reputations of those who were there. I found this to be a rare work of survival told with a truthful immediacy that leaves the reader stunned but not numbed. It is not easy reading, but urgent reading, recommended reading.

Michael Berenbaum
Director, Sigi Ziering Institute: Exploring the Ethical and Religious Implications of the Holocaust
Professor of Theology
The University of Judaism
Los Angeles, California

4

Book review

Great book for the classroom. Examines vividly the horrors of the Holocaust through the innocent eyes of a child. A roller-coaster of a ride that takes the reader on a journey that describes the love of a family forced to combat the evils of both the Nazi and of the neighbor. It is a child's account of fear, of guilt, of despair, of destruction, of senseless death, and even of the existence of G-d. Events and issues so familiar to the student of today (post-9/11). I strongly advise every educator and student of the Shoah to use this book. It will challenge the reader never to forget and to make a difference ... a story of good over evil that will truly inspire!

Carl F. Munson
Educator
Lockport, Illinois

Book review

Aaron Elster's haunting memoir is so compelling that it becomes difficult not to place oneself in his shoes. For young readers, Aaron's emotionally gripping narrative can be a powerful tool for conveying the atrocities of the Holocaust in a most personal way.

Aaron's experiences during his childhood provide a glimpse of what one innocent young boy endured during World War II. We read of Aaron's choices and sacrifices, and how he worked tirelessly to survive the evil of the Nazis' war against the Jews.

It is stories such as Aaron's that will be conveyed in the new Illinois Holocaust Museum and Education Center, now under construction in Skokie. It is because of courageous people like Aaron Elster that the organizers of the new Center are so anxious to bring this project to fruition. Aaron's commitment and devotion to the new museum, and to telling his story of survival, is inspiring to us all.

Richard S. Hirschhaut
Project and Executive Director
Illinois Holocaust Museum and Education Center
Skokie, Illinois

6

Book reviews

An unforgettable, moving meditation of a hidden child during the Holocaust and his reckoning with unbearable memories through sheer determination, the goodness of others, and the drive to bear witness. Through his eloquent speaking and writing, Aaron Elster has completed the voyage from the solitary hidden child in the attic to successful executive to inspiring educator.

Leon Stein
Professor, Roosevelt University, Illinois

This is a powerful and inspiring story of a child's survival against all odds during the Holocaust. It is told in the child's authentic voice and is full of vivid and arresting details and unforgettable scenes. Aaron Elster's story is a testimony to the strength and resiliency of the human spirit. He courageously continues to relate it in person to teach youngsters about the consequences of hatred and bigotry.

Elliot Lefkovitz
Professor, Loyola University
Chicago, Illinois

Chapters

Dedication

From Aaron Elster:

My deepest appreciation to all those who encouraged me to pursue the writing of my story. First, to the love of my life, Jackie, who was the first woman to ever say she loved me, and who has been my constant encouragement; my son Bob, who helped me formulate my story; my son Steve, for helping me organize all the details; my granddaughters, Sarah and Allison, who are the jewels in my life that fill my heart with love with their smiles and their mere presence; to my sister Irene, and to the hero in my life, my uncle Sam Scherb.

Gene Walsh, Rick Hirschhaut and Kelley Szany from the Holocaust Memorial Foundation; the thousands of students who wanted to know more about my life and asked me to write my story; Monica Vest Wheeler for her dedication and hard work; Fritzie Fritzshall who brought Joy Miller into my life and made this a reality; and Joy Miller, who did for me what I haven't been able to accomplish in many years. I will forever be grateful.

And this book is dedicated to the memory of my mother and father, whose lives were cut short by a world filled with hatred. They were so proud of their children. And my baby sister Sara, I will never forget you. Now, all who read "our" story will carry your soul with them to eternity.

Dedication

From Joy Erlichman Miller, Ph.D.:

Sometimes the Universe brings things into your life at just the right moment. When I met Aaron, I knew we were brought together for a purpose. It has been my honor to share his story and ensure that it is never forgotten. His strength and endurance is a testimony to the resiliency of the human spirit in the face of adversity.

Special thanks to my editor and friend, Monica Vest Wheeler, who made this beautiful text come alive. Your talent and dedication to preserving history are miracles from your heart.

Thanks to Fritzie Fritzshall for bringing Aaron into my life, and being a mentoring force in my life. And to my loving husband John, who always encourages me, and is the wind that sets my life free to pursue dreams.

May this work honor the memory of all those who lost their lives during the Holocaust ... with the hope that it will serve as a witness to all those who dare to speak out against intolerance, prejudice and bigotry.

10

Why We Created This Book

This book was built on a foundation of compassion. Trust constructed the walls; love applied the roof.

Aaron Elster appeared in Peoria, Illinois, in May 2006 at the annual Yom HaShoah (Holocaust Remembrance) event, sponsored by the Jewish Federation of Peoria. Aaron and I had met a few years before through a mutual friend, Holocaust survivor Fritzie Fritzshall, but we began communicating almost daily in preparation for his presentation at our temple/synagogue.

Aaron connected with everyone that evening in the packed room. Many shed tears upon hearing his story. His voice and informal style captivated each person. I listened and cried along with everyone else, but there was something unique about Aaron's story: it was filled with the emotions of a 10-year-old. This survivor story was a special moving experience that touched my heart in so many ways.

I was profoundly moved by and drawn to Aaron and his life. I wanted to help him put his story down on paper. It needed to be something that would captivate readers as much as it had his listeners. I decided that I would do whatever it took to make this, his dream of publishing his story, a reality. Aaron and I spent countless hours together discussing his life, the tragedies and triumphs, and the very core of what turned this boy into a Holocaust survivor, his unfathomable resiliency.

My insatiable hunger to learn from him and his need to reach out and teach created the voice of this volume: the perspective of the 10-year-old boy whose world was under

siege more than six decades ago. It's because the little boy still lingers inside the man, and that is true of all of us, that we never forget the pain that tears at us from within. However, we can all learn from those scars and become better and stronger individuals, and leave an indescribable impact on the world.

That is the message of this book.

Joy Erlichman Miller, Ph.D.

O nly guard yourself
and guard your soul
carefully, lest you forget
the things your eyes saw, and
lest these things depart your
heart all the days of your life.
And you shall make them
known to your children and
your children's children.

Deuteronomy 4:9

Part One:
My World Changes

Chapter 1
Entering Hell

On a brisk October morning, I quickly walk through the immense parking lot of the Chicago suburban high school. Checking the time, I notice the bright sunlight reflect off my watch, sending a spectrum of light in various directions. I hurry my pace, not wanting to be late for my speaking engagement. Rehearsing my speech in my head as I near the high school entrance, I try to concentrate on the important aspects I want to emphasize. Despite my efforts, my mind seems unable to fully concentrate. This makes me somewhat anxious and fearful.

Instantly, I realize today is October 10, and I feel an intense cold sensation, an internal shiver that creeps outward and attacks my skin. I was once told that the body holds memories deep within itself. I can't ignore the memory that over 60 years ago, on this very day, my life changed and I entered the hell known as the Holocaust.

Scanning my environment, I detect a disturbing, unsettling feeling inside of me. An intense ache twists my stomach, and dizziness threatens to attack me. My throat suddenly feels like continuous breathing will soon become impossible. My heart hammers in a way similar to the sensations that I experienced during my heart attack years ago. My palms become so wet that I almost drop my brown leather briefcase.

I try to straighten up and regain my composure, but the air feels thin, and it is challenging to maintain my balance. I struggle to reorient myself and focus my eyes upon the high school entrance, now seemingly out of reach. Filled with overwhelming anxiety, I'm losing the battle against this panic attack. I'm sure I will not be able to complete my task of lecturing 1,200 students about the Holocaust.

Attempting to put one foot in front of the other, I'm now distracted by a pungent scent of smoke. It is a mixture of something that smells like rotting or deterioration. Perhaps it is the stench of fall, nature dying. Whatever it is, its powerful aroma complicates the struggle to maintain my balance. I have the terrifying sensation of everything closing in on me.

I must get inside the high school. Then everything will be okay. My pace toward the building accelerates, but I'm captured by the past, unable to escape its hold.

Chapter 2
October 10, 1942

On this morning of Yom Kippur, my mother fran-
ticly pushes me as everyone runs to the hiding
place. Moments ago I was sound asleep and
unaware of this secret location. Now I am being herded to
a second floor apartment in our building within the ghetto. Shoved against the others, I see a door pried open, creating a passageway for our anxious group.

I feel the bodies of our neighbors crashing into my
own. I hear the screams and crying, and the fear takes a
devilish hold on each person. Mothers and fathers fever-
ishly assist the young children and elderly into a square
opening hidden by a crudely designed wooden cover so
that it seems that nothing exists behind this wall. Inside
this space, I see a ladder that everyone tries at once to
descend into a secret room. Mothers grasp babies in their
arms as more than three dozen try to squeeze into a room
the size of an average bedroom.

When we all gain access into the hidden room, a man
reaches up and grabs the ladder and places it flat on the
floor. I'm shaking and trying to hold back my tears. All I
can feel is intense fear, and I realize more than anything
that I don't want to die. My father urges me to sit next to
him as he pulls my baby sister Sara close to me. Dressed
in short pants, I crouch down on the dirt floor. My body
begins to shake in uncontrollable convulsions.

To my right, I notice a little window that looks over the
street. Peeking through it, I watch my neighbors below
being chased by Ukrainian guards, cursing as they bludg-
eon their victims with rubber bats and whips. Wildly try-

ing to escape the punishing blows, a young woman runs with one of my school friends down the small hill from Rogofska Street to the back of our house on Piekna Street. How can these horrors be possible when the sun is shining so brilliantly on such a beautiful fall day?

I look around for my mother, but all I see are my neighbors trying to shield and protect their own families. Two disheveled old men stand against the wall mumbling prayers to G-d, as others quietly whisper to each other that G-d doesn't exist because He does not hear our people's prayers. Another old man with a graying beard invokes the Lord's name as he strains to utter the holy words of dedication to our faith reciting the Shema Yisrael, but G-d does not appear to hear.

Sara begins to whimper as she nestles closer to our father, whose face reveals terror and dismay. Our father looks down and tells her she must be totally silent, or we will be discovered. I see a young mother breast-feeding her baby, and suddenly there is an outburst from another infant across the crowded room.

The captives tell the young mother to silence the baby, but the noise continues. The elders insist that the mother must quiet the infant's outbursts, or they fear the Gestapo will discover us and we will all be murdered. The urging continues as the baby's cries become louder and louder as the onlookers become more agitated and anxious.

My eyes must be deceiving me as the distraught mother places her palm over her daughter's mouth and nose and exerts pressure. The baby's legs begin to violently flail and kick until they move no more. Silence fills the room as the infant takes her final gasp for air and suddenly goes limp.

Tears fill my eyes, and instantly I wonder if my mother would do the same to me in such an impulsive action. I watch, but I feel little emotion related to the death. I only feel relief that we will not be discovered. Looking up at

I Still See Her Haunting Eyes

18 my father, as my body continues to shake in terror, it is clear that no one will say anything about the mother's actions. Holding back a sickening need to throw up, I place my face under my father's arm as my teeth begin to chatter.

Inside me, all I witness is my deepening fear, and I am consumed with the powerful desire to live in spite of what I have just seen. I don't want to die, and I'm scared of the pain that must come when there is death. I pray for G-d to spare me, but why would He save me, for I am not worthy of saving.

Now I hear loud footsteps. Crashing sounds fill the air. The intense noise shatters the silence as the wooden square is ripped from the ceiling that protects us. A demonic face appears and vanishes. Gunshots shatter the safety of our surroundings. All of a sudden the room is filled with screams of *"Raus, raus!"* (*Out, out!*)

From their location over the wooden door, the invaders scream that we are dirty Jews and call us dogs and vermin. The shattering noise of the bullets echoes in my ears, and part of me goes numb inside. Suddenly, there are motionless people all around me. Some appear dead with blood pouring onto the floor. I realize that blood now fills my mouth. A bullet hit the wall, and a giant wood splinter is imbedded in my upper lip. Removing the wood, I touch my lip and taste the blood upon my finger, and a part of me goes deeper into myself. I can see what is happening around me, but my emotions go dead. I watch silently and pray.

We have no choice ... we must exit this place and face our perpetrators. With screams filling the room, I watch my neighbors climb up the ladder that takes us from our hiding place. My dad ascends the ladder holding little Sara in his arms. I climb behind him into the world filled with the devils of hatred. My father's back shields me from the blows of the Ukrainian guard who screams obscenities and laughs as I stumble to get to my feet.

Young and old are beaten with rubber bats as the Ukrainians chase us to the hallway walls. Those who do not move quickly enough are beaten, and an old woman who moves too slowly is shot in the head. I watch her crumple in her own blood. Another woman is hurled against the wall, and I look for my mother, but she is gone. Then I catch sight of a guard pulling her down the hallway and taking her away from us.

My father grabs my arm, and Sara cries as she holds onto my father's coat. I try to look down, and I dare not look at these men even for one moment. Perhaps if I just look down on the ground, I will become invisible. Don't look into their eyes, no matter what. I pray they will not see me. My body shakes once again, and I pray I will awaken from this awful nightmare.

Shoved from the hallway of our building, we are pushed into the street filled with chaotic screaming and cries of pain. I survey the ghetto that was once our home. The dead lay on the cobbled street as Ukrainian soldiers, police and the Gestapo orchestrate our march towards the Market Place in the middle of town. People around me are being dragged from their houses, beaten and clubbed.

As we are chased into the Market, an old lady, unable to keep pace with the rest, falls. The guards do not stoop to pick her up. Instead these monsters kick her over and over until she lies mangled on the ground dead. The men laugh and sneer as they walk away, and once again I keep my eyes to the ground, convinced they may not see me. As the cries echo, the survivors are gathered and led to the Market Place on Rogofska Street. I tremble and realize we will all be taken to the gas chambers or a death camp.

Please, I don't want to die! A Gestapo guard points a machine gun at all of us and I look to the sky and wonder if G-d really exists.

Europe with Sokolow, Poland marked with the star.

Chapter 3
1940: Our World and Theirs

My name is Aaron (Aron) Elster. I am eight years old, and my world is different now. It's 1940 and I live in Sokolow, Podlaski, in the open ghetto with my father Chaim Sruel Elster, mother Cywia, older sister Irene (Ita), who is 11, and baby sister Sara (Sura) Rivka, who is only four years old.

My father is tall and lanky, which makes his pants and jacket hang on his slender stature. His hair is usually cut short with touches of grey that contrast with his rugged and long face and deep-set eyes.

My mother is a beauty. Her hair is raven black, which compliments her round full face. Most people tend to stare at my mother because she is so strikingly attractive. I've overheard rumors that my mother was very popular as a teenager, and it was said that my parents' marriage was arranged, which is the custom of my town. I heard my aunt whisper that my mother was forced to marry my father by her domineering father, because my father's family was financially secure. All I know is that I never see my parents kiss or show affection with each other.

My older sister Irene is much taller than me, and she has my mother's black hair and attractiveness. Her brown eyes seem to sparkle when she laughs. My precious little sister Sara has a smile that lights up a room. She always has her hair in two pigtails that swing from side to side every time she moves her head. I always like spending time with Sara because she is so innocent and loving, and giggles a lot when I talk to her.

Aaron's maternal grandparents, Mordechai and Masha
Scherb, and his aunt Fina.

Aaron's father,
Chaim Sruel
Elster

Our house is located on a cobblestone pavement on Piekna Street. It's part of a red wooden building that houses our apartment as well as six other tenants. One of my uncles, who is a Rabbi, lives in our building. This is also the location of the Heder (religious school) that I attend. We enter our apartment through a kitchen that holds a large wood-burning stove with four burners we use for cooking and warming our home. Large metal pots and pans hang from the ceiling in our kitchen, and their reflection always seems to shine down on the hutch that holds our everyday dishes.

Each Friday, Irene, Sara and I take our weekly bath, and all three of us get in one big wooden tub that is filled with hot water that has been warmed on the stove. While

24

Aaron's mother, Cywia (Scherb) Elster

we are bathing my mother warms a blanket on the oven, and then wraps us each up in the wonderfully heated blanket as she takes us into the bedroom to sleep. This is one of my favorite family rituals, even though I complain about taking a bath.

My family all sleeps together in one large bedroom. There are two oversized beds that are next to each other on one side of the room. My father and I sleep in one bed, and I always feel safe having him next to me. Right by my bed, we have a door that leads to the outside.

My mother sleeps alone in the bed next to ours. Sara's baby bed is nestled next to my mother's, and sometimes I watch Sara as she sleeps. Irene has her own bed on the other side of the room, by the curtained windows. I'm thankful I don't have to sleep alone and can enjoy the comfort of being by my father's side.

The whole house has shiny wood floors, and carpets decorate our apartment. There is a large round table, with a special tablecloth made of lace. On top of the wooden table rest some beautiful display items, but we only use this table for special occasions or for holidays like Passover or Yom Kippur (Jewish Day of Atonement).

Outside our house we have a garden, and I love to watch my father plant carrots, cucumbers, onions and sunflowers. He seems to delight in watching them grow, as do I. Next to our garden is the outhouse. Irene is scared to go outside alone at night and use the outhouse, so I go with her, but she always has to give me something special to be her nighttime bathroom chaperone. Sometimes I run inside, and she gets really mad that I have left her alone out in the backyard in the dark with the cow.

Sometimes I pass the time by playing soccer. When I play outside, I imagine I am all grown up and very strong. A month or so ago, I made an amazing trade, giving up my unwanted dessert for a toy wooden rifle made by my older cousin. I feel strong and tough when I carry this toy made from a wooden shingle cut in the shape of a mighty weapon. The rifle is so wonderful; it even has a way to shoot a pretend arrow. It is my constant companion in my neighborhood activities, and I imagine I have a way to protect myself from any harm that might become me.

The dining room table is the center of all activities in our home, and all the rumors and conversations about our future as Jews are discussed here. I sit on the floor against the wall listening to the adults.

Sometimes our neighbor Gedala visits our apartment, and I am terrified listening to his stories. Something about him scares me, and my intuition tells me to stay far away from him whenever he enters our home.

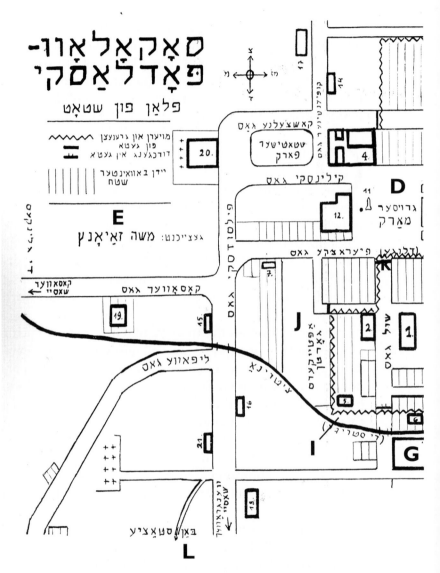

A detailed drawing of the Jewish ghetto in Sokolow, Poland. Aaron's family lived on **Piekna Street**, and the family meat market was on **Rogofska Street.** *(Memorial Book of Sokolow-Podlaski)*

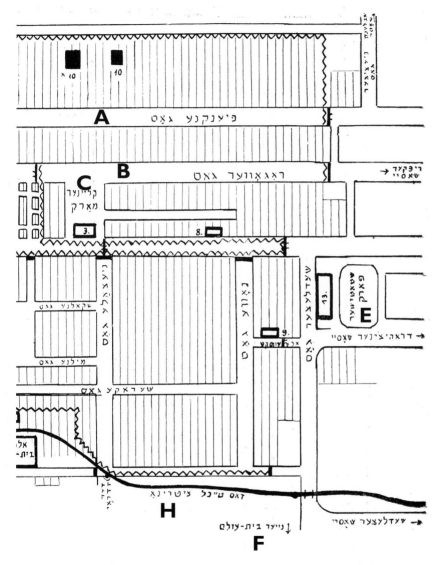

Key to map

A: Piekna Street
B: Rogofska Street
C: Small market
D: Large market
E: City park
F: New cemetery
G: Old cemetery
H: River
I: Ghetto walls
J: Pharmacist's garden
K: Temple Street
L: Train station

I Still See Her Haunting Eyes

28 Gedala is a German Jew who was driven into Poland. He predicts that we will soon be stripped of our possessions, our family business, and that someday soon we will be taken to labor camps or worse yet, be exterminated. I don't know what exterminated means, but I know we exterminate bugs in our pantry, so it must be something horrid. Whenever these conversations begin, I stare out the small curtained window and fade into my own world where I am safe from harm.

Our town, Sokolow, is located 80 kilometers east of Warsaw, Poland, in the Lublin Province. By the beginning of the 20th century, our Jewish settlement had grown in great proportions. Traders and crafters are the main source of income for the region, with our 5,000 Jewish residents taking on occupations such as butchers like my parents, tailors, shoemakers, furriers, bakers, and blacksmiths. Our world also has some industrial types of businesses, like a Jewish-owned flour mill, a print factory, and a brick factory that employs many of us within the ghetto area.

There are two separate worlds within this small town: Their world and ours. Our Jewish world is comprised of several streets, which surround the main synagogue. In our world, traditional Jewish culture thrives. A yeshiva, a school for religious learning, is attended by almost 150 students from our town and surrounding areas. We have many other schools, which include Jewish kindergartens, Talmud Torah schools and Heders, like the one I attend.

Our world contains a Jewish theatre, a widely read Jewish newspaper, two Jewish libraries, and numerous political and social organizations that are attended by many people in our community. During Shabbat (Friday night and Saturday religious observance of the Sabbath), the town bustles with so many religious observers that the synagogue overflows with attendees.

Mother Cywia and sister Sara, right, and cousin Hannah, left. This is the only known photo of Aaron's sister Sara.

I Still See Her Haunting Eyes

30 Their world is outside the open ghetto and comprises most of the town. Their world has almost twice as many people as we have within our world. We are allowed to enter their world, but sometimes it is dangerous. They don't really like people from our world, and sometimes call us vile names such as "Christ killers" or *szwinia* (pigs). We are seen as lower class citizens of Poland, and anti-Semitism is quite common. It seems we've always been hated in their world for one reason or another. We are allowed to pass into their world and purchase food from neighboring farmers, but we are always very cautious.

Our two worlds come together on Thursdays when the Market Place, off Dluga Street, is filled with the neighboring farmers and traders who sell their goods throughout the day. Beginning early in the morning, the Market Place becomes the scene of constant activity. Everywhere there is something different to purchase or look at. Horse-drawn wagons stuffed with fresh produce and grains fill the area. Stands are filled with tools, cloth, supplies, livestock and handcrafted goods of all kinds. The Market Place is filled with the odor of manure and aromas of fruits and vegetables mingling in the air.

Everyone in Sokolow joins in the festivities of this anticipated weekly event. The days are warm, and the sounds and smells of the market welcome people from both worlds. Bartering and trading continue for most of the day, and the atmosphere is almost circus-like, which creates a holiday feeling for everyone in our town. I find myself wishing Thursdays would last forever.

My parents own a butcher shop located in the Market Place called Rynek, on Rogofska Street. A hand-painted sign hangs over the entrance doors with a picture of a quarter of meat and a meat cleaver. My mother works in her short sheep coat and converses with the customers. She always weighs the order and then gives each person an extra piece of meat or bone at no additional cost.

The Sokolow Market Place. *(Memorial Book of Sokolow-Podlaski)*

I Still See Her Haunting Eyes

Our butcher shop is somewhat unique because we sell our meats to the Gentile (non-Jewish) population, which means we sell meat that is not kosher (meat that came from animals not slaughtered according to Jewish law). This is somewhat uncomfortable because the Jews see us as not pious if we eat any of the meat we sell. The non-Jews purchase food from us, but sometimes angry young Poles protest in front of our store and condemn people who enter our business to purchase goods. The Polish hooligans slap signs on the backs of customers as they exit our butcher shop. The signs ridicule them for doing business with "Jewish pigs." I don't understand why we are hated, because I can't remember doing anything to hurt anyone.

Earlier this year I was walking down the street with a boy whose father was named Surdik, named by the Nazis as the Commander of the Jewish Ghetto Police. I don't remember the beginning of the conversation, but all of the sudden his eyes filled with anger, and he screamed something about me being a "Christ killer." I must have looked frightened and confused, because I didn't even know who Christ was, and for sure I hadn't killed him. He kept pointing his finger close to my eyes and demanding an immediate answer why I had killed his savior. It felt like he wanted to kill me for something I didn't do.

Petrified, I ran home telling my parents about being accused of killing some man named Christ. I wish my mother would have hugged me and told me I did not have to be scared, but she sternly told me to stay away from the Polish boys, and that they hated us for doing something we did not do. She said the Poles believed we were the cause of their sorrows and agony. From that day on, I knew we were hated for being falsely accused of doing something that could never be changed.

All my life I've lived with them hating us; it's just a fact of life. Somehow they have the idea that we killed their Lord and call us names that really hurt my feelings. Somehow they have the idea that we capture their children to use their blood to make Matzoh for our Passover Seder (meal). I remember watching my mother make Matzoh, but I've never seen anyone kill any children during its preparation.

I'm just confused hearing these strange misconceptions, but realize I am in danger for being born a Jew. All I know is that Polish boys chase me and try to beat me, so I know it is not safe to walk alone in our town.

Things seemed to be getting worse for all of the Jews in Sokolow in the last six months. I still remember the Germans invading our town as the Red Army retreated into the Soviet-occupied zone of Poland. Thundering noises filled the air with heavy bombers. Many families escaped into the nearby forests and for the first time I experienced intense terror and fear. This was when my preoccupation with avoiding pain and death began.

The Gendarmes (police officials) and the German soldiers are everywhere. Their high black boots and steel helmets are a frightening sight. The soldiers are cruel monsters who abuse my neighbors without cause. Sometimes they capture the elders and take scissors and cut their beards, and then ridicule them in public as they call them vile names. Some of the Polish boys call me a *"parsziwi zyd"* (filthy kike) and say *"Zydzi, Zydzi zatobom Hitler idzje"* (Jew, Jew, Hitler is after you).

Now we are forced to move off the sidewalks when a German soldier walks nearby, and I keep my eyes on the ground. I notice my stomach begins to ache whenever I see these scary men. The German soldiers randomly grab people off the street, and we never see them again.

One night, without warning, three frightening German police enter our home and drag my father out of our house. The tall red-haired Gendarme is a vicious man who everyone fears because he appears to enjoy beating people at will. He scares me in his long green coat and matching green steel helmet adorned with a swastika. He has a large bayonet on one side of his immense brown leather belt, and on the other side of his body rests a silver revolver.

Quickly, our mother holds Irene, Sara and me against the walls of our apartment as my father attempts to fight off the attackers. We've done nothing to cause this invasion, but I scream as we watch the police beat my father with a long wooden pole across his arms and back. Breaking his arm, they drag him into a group of others who are to be sent to slave labor, but somehow my father escapes and makes his way back to the ghetto.

After my father's return home, we begin to hear rumors from the Poles who frequent our butcher shop. They tell us this beating is a warning to remind us that we must pay off the Poles and the Germans for doing business in "their" town. From that day forward, it is clear that we must deliver food or money to the police who expect a weekly payoff for their protection. I constantly pray that G-d will save me and my family from these awful men who seem to hate us.

On another night two drunken men in filthy clothes are pounding on our door. The men pull my father outside by his neck and threaten to kill him. These Polish men can do whatever they want because we have no rights as Jews. We are not allowed to own guns to protect ourselves.

As I watch with my sister Irene, my mother runs outside and gives the attackers some money. The two men laugh and throw down their bottles of liquor smashing into little pieces. The men take the money from my mother and run away. I told my mother that I remember these two men coming to our meat market to buy goods, but she told me that we could never trust anyone who is not Jewish. Now I'm scared of every Gentile that I see.

Most recently, my 16-year-old uncle Label was brutally tortured by the Gestapo. One night, Uncle Label was caught in part of a Gestapo round up with hundreds of other men and placed in a cattle car being sent to a slave labor camp. Having heard the predictions of what happened to captured Jews, Label jumped from the moving cattle car. He landed on the ground, but was shot in the neck by a German guard as he attempted to escape. Label kept running and hid in the woods for a short time.

Somehow Uncle Label made his way back to Sokolow and he returned to our apartment building. It was such a grotesque sight because the bullet had entered his neck, leaving a big hole, and exited the other side penetrating his arm. Each day I heard Uncle Label shriek in pain, and the wounds became infected and filled with pus.

No one from outside our building would help him, because he was now an escaped criminal. Uncle Label died in our home, and now I have nightmares about death and the pain that is associated with killing. Sometimes I cry in my sleep, and I always think about Label's bloodied body. I often lay awake all night trying to feel safe laying next to my father.

I try to talk to my parents about what is happening, but they assure me that we will be okay, and that I don't need to worry. I try to believe what they tell me, but I really am having a hard time believing we are safe. I think they are just saying this to help us sleep at night, and I think they are hoping these words of assurance will end my nightmares.

Our world is beginning to crumble before my eyes. I just know that I don't want to die.

I Still See Her Haunting Eyes

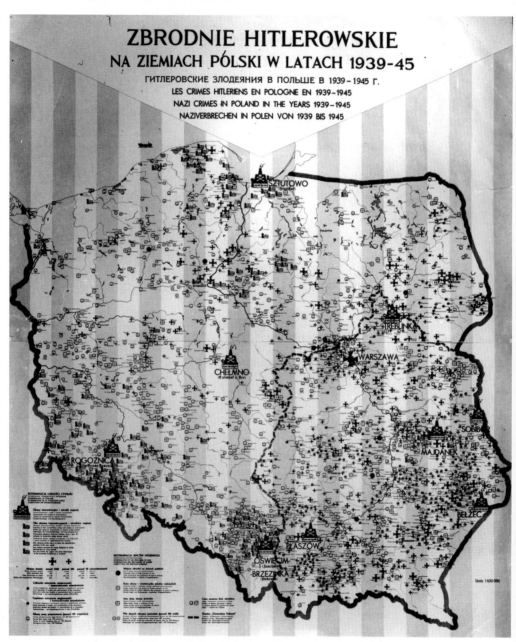

A map showing Nazi crimes in Poland from 1939-45.
(Photo courtesy Yad Vashem Film and Photo Archive)

Chapter 4
A Life Filled With Fear

F ear is my constant companion. I find myself always looking around, glancing behind me and watching, always watching. I hang onto every unknown sound, and I am easily startled, thinking that someone is coming to kill me. I walk slowly around corners because I never know what's hiding out of sight. My muscles tense as if I am always ready to flee.

I don't think the tension in my body lets go even when I try to sleep. My heart always seems to be racing, and I know that my mind always focuses on pain, killings, fires and death. Trembling joins panic, as I always live feeling uneasy and anxious. I have constant thoughts about the future of my family, and most often I have dreadful visions of being murdered and the pain I feel when I am killed. I feel guilty that I spend so much time thinking only of myself.

Even when I sleep, I have vivid nightmares. Blazing fires are a common symbol reminding me of the riots that broke out on Pesah (Passover) a few years ago during a Polish pogrom. In my torment I relive witnessing our local stores and markets being set on fire as the non-Jews stand by idly and watch. In my horrid dreams these Gentiles all wear scary red and black masks that frighten me, and I hear their taunting laughter as the town begins to burn out of control. Other times in my nightmares, I see the inferno of flames as our synagogue burns to the ground.

Sometimes I have bad dreams about what has really happened, like the night when the German army entered

I Still See Her Haunting Eyes

our town in September 1939, and how they set our holy place on fire. Our Torah (holy scrolls) burned in the raging fire, and no one was allowed to enter the building to save our religious artifacts, or they would be killed on the spot. As the fires raged, our chief Rabbi was pulled from the Yeshiva and forced to dance near the town square. The shadows of his body faded into the billowing black smoke that surrounded the flaming synagogue. G-d watched, but He did not put out the flames. In my nightmares I see the fire, and G-d looks down from His clouds and then looks away.

I have more nightmares about other things that happened in 1939 when the Germans invaded Sokolow. My

The new large synagogue, which was later destroyed by the Nazis. *(Memorial Book of Sokolow-Podlaski)*

I Still See Her Haunting Eyes

dreams revisit the horrors as the Nazis entered our holy little synagogue at Maly Rynek, just as evening services were being conducted. These monsters smashed the door and began wildly shooting their guns into the air, hitting the ceiling of the small synagogue. The bullets flew throughout the sanctuary, and one innocent woman, who was praying for G-d's protection, was murdered in cold blood. From that day forward, many prayed in secret within their homes or any place they would not be noticed.

In my dreams I see myself running from those bullets as they bounce off the walls and come towards my head. I look up to G-d, and the bullet always strikes me in my dream. I begin screaming in pain, and then I awake. Each time I awake I am uncontrollably trembling, sweaty, and sure this will be my destiny. But no one comforts me and tells me everything will be all right.

The fear is so great inside me. My stomach is always upset, and it feels uneasy like I'm going to throw up. Food is very scarce and daily ration portions determined by the German Reich are very small. My mother has become very worried about me and tells me I must eat or I will die. It seems I will die, no matter what happens.

One day my mother brings me into our back yard, and she pulls a *kielbasa* (sausage) from a pocket of the large beige coat she was wearing. She tells me I must eat the sausage, and not to tell anyone that I was eating something that was not kosher. Nervously I eat the sausage, which is delicious, but I am sure I will go to Hell for my actions.

The thoughts of never being able to enter Heaven are constant because of my religious training. My Rabbi, clothed in a long black coat and his contrasting long red beard, assures me that there is a ladder that leads up to Heaven. He says if I break a commandment or commit a sin, a rung is taken out of the ladder and I will no longer be able to climb to Heaven. His message runs through my

40

Photos of children in the Sokolow Jewish ghetto in 1942. The men in the top photograph are wearing Stars of David on their sleeves. *(Photo courtesy Yad Vashem Film and Photo Archive)*

mind as I visualize him saying that my soul will wander for eternity and never find peace. I eat the sausage given to me by my mother, but I'm now destined to live in Hell. I'm sure all of my unspeakable acts will insure that G-d will not save me from harm.

As time passes, it becomes increasingly difficult for my family to maintain the butcher shop. The Germans have turned their backs, and we are allowed to continue to stay in business, but only if we pay off those in command. Each week someone comes to our store and collects a ransom or payment, which allows us to keep our butcher shop open. My mother saves money, and reluctantly gives the Gendarmes money fearing we will be harmed.

I worry about what will happen to us if we do not have money to pay off the monsters. Irene sneaks outside the ghetto and delivers meat to the Poles. This is one of the only ways we can deliver food to some of our customers who are fearful of entering our store and being seen as a "Jew-lover." My father assists Irene as she exits the ghetto, easily assimilating into "their" world because she does not look Jewish. But what if Irene is caught? What if we are all captured and killed?

But life begins to change again, and everything is different.

Chapter 5
Trapped Within the Ghetto

I'm now nine, and it is 1941. The German soldiers are everywhere. They scare me. Things are changing in our ghetto. After the German invasion of the Soviet Union on June 22, 1941, things got worse for us. Our ghetto is now going to be "closed." This means we can no longer go to school or outside of the ghetto area. We are totally closed off from all the non-Jews in Sokolow. If we go against the new rules, we will be killed on the spot or sent to a labor camp.

A Polish engineer named Bonk begins to measure the streets and develops a plan to close the ghetto. I watch as all the Jewish men are forced to erect a large wall around the small area. The wall is very high, and it is closed at the end by a large wooden gate that is guarded all the time by the police.

If that isn't bad enough, they put very sharp razor barbed wire on the top of the wall, and then they make the men put broken glass up there to cut us if we try to escape. I constantly think of how terrible and painful it would be to be cut by those barbed wires that look like razors. Sometimes I have nightmares of what they feel like against my skin.

The ghetto has a six-member Judenrat that has been chosen by the Germans. This group is told that it will be responsible for the functions of police and fire protection, food distribution, and housing. Many of the Jewish leaders are very uncomfortable with creating a Judenrat, but there are no exceptions. The German orders must be followed.

The group of Jewish men, lead by Lewin, has been instructed to perform certain duties in our town, in hopes of saving all who live here. The Germans have promised the Judenrat that we will be safe if we follow the orders they place on all Jews to the exact letter of the law. Erman, who is a Gestapo official, has told the Judenrat that if they collect money from the Jewish population, our ghetto will remain a work ghetto and be protected. We have heard that the Jews from neighboring towns of Siedlece, Wengrow and Koscow are also being put in closed ghettos.

Last year, the Judenrat was ordered to begin picking men to be sent to work in slave labor camps. Everyone fears being placed on this new deadly list. My parents paid money to the Judenrat and arranged to have my

Announcement of the creation of the Ghetto in Sokolow.
(Memorial Book of Sokolow-Podlaski)

44 dad's name taken off the list. Each week more and more people are being sent to the slave camp that is located by Korczon, which is about 15 kilometers south of our town. Some Jews elect to go the slave camp because the food rations are larger, and they believe they will have a better chance to live.

Around the outside of the closed ghetto are police who ensure we do not exit our prison. The head of the Jewish Ghetto police is a Pole named Surdik, whose son had called me a "Christ killer" only two years ago. Inside the walls of the ghetto, we are ruled by Gestapo police orders, which are carried out by the Judenrat and the Ghetto Police. The Jewish police do not carry guns, but they have huge black batons they wear on their large belts, and we know to abide by whatever they tell us.

Our area is also getting more crowded because the Germans have placed 2,000 refugees from places like Lodz and Kalisz inside our little ghetto area. These Jewish refugees lived in surrounding farms or in the countryside. Now three or four families are forced to live in one apartment. There are lots of people who are very hungry and are lying on the streets begging for food. There are children who are propped up against the walls of the buildings, and they cry and beg people to give them some food.

I've never seen anything like this before. These people look somewhat like skeletons with clothes. Disease is spreading, and many people are catching something called typhus. I can't look in their eyes because it reminds me of my nightmares of death.

Our house was always located inside the ghetto area, so we are able to continue to live in our home. However, the Germans have mandated that those Jews in the *generalgouvernement* (those places of Poland not directly annexed to Germany that held some 2 million Jews) are to be placed on a rationing card system. We are only allowed to get food that is well below what is needed for daily life. Because food is becoming more difficult to obtain, my mother says we need to make sure that we don't waste any of the food that we have hidden in our cellar. My parents are very concerned because we were forced to close our butcher shop, which was located in the ghetto area.

On some days we are able to buy some food from the black market inside the ghetto, but it is very costly and dangerous to access. This is accomplished by making a deal with Poles who arrange for the exchange of goods. These black market deals occur at the barbed wire fence at a prearranged date and time. These dealings could mean death to anyone who is seen by the police or Gestapo. Of course, the guards could also be bribed to look the other way, as corruption is a part of daily life in the ghetto. Despite the risk, my mother uses our small savings or barters with the Poles with some of our valuables in exchange for food.

Ukrainian and German soldiers pushing an old Jewish man to the Market Place. *(Memorial Book of Sokolow-Podlaski)*

I Still See Her Haunting Eyes

Yesterday I heard my parents talking at the dining room table. My mother said she knows some ways to smuggle in some meat from a farmer outside our area, but they say we will have to pay a huge amount of money to obtain the food. I'm not sure how they are going to do this, but I pray at night that they will not be caught and sent away, but mostly I pray that I will not die from hunger.

The town I once knew is now changed. Everything is different. There is human waste and garbage thrown on the streets. I walk along the street by the small Market Place, at the edge of the ghetto, and see dead bodies piled in this huge pyramid. The smell is something I cannot describe. Some days they pick up dead bodies and throw them in a giant pit, which is like a big grave. They throw these dead bodies, that were once people we knew, into these giant holes, like the people are just garbage on the street. It terrifies me to go outside alone.

Everyone is forced to wear a Jewish Star of David, which is sewn on his or her clothes or worn on a white armband with a blue star. This is a German law that is strictly enforced. The yellow star must always be on our clothing, or we will be sent to a labor camp or murdered on the spot. This order to wear a Star upon our clothes at all times makes it impossible to try to hide, because everyone can pick us out from Poles.

We are like inmates in a prison with barbed wire holding us in like cattle or pigs. I keep trying to make a deal with G-d and promise Him I will do anything He wants, if He lets us live.

In my dreams I fantasize that I escape from this place and that I am not being hunted down like a wild animal, just for being born a Jew. I wake up screaming because I'm sure there is something sinful about hating that I was born Jewish. I know G-d will never save me from this awful place, and I know I will be forced to die a painful bloody death.

Besides, there is no way that I could hide because it is very easy to tell if a boy is Jewish or not. When the boy or man disrobes, the observer can immediately tell if we are Jews by our circumcision. This religious ritual is a blessed ceremony, which is performed only on Jewish males, and makes it impossible to hide our identity. I hate being born a male and a Jew, and for this I feel ashamed.

I cannot stop thinking about what is happening to us. I always pray to G-d, and ask Him to save us. Why do we have to die? What did we do? What terrible sins did we commit? Why do the Germans hate us so much? Why are so many Ukrainians and the Poles helping them? But my questions to G-d are never answered.

And my world changes, again.

Chapter 6
My Life is Forever Changed

It's 1942, and I am 10 years old. Things are getting much worse in our town. The Germans have brought lots of Ukrainian soldiers here. These men terrify me because I've seen them bayonet some of the people in our ghetto for no reason.

One day I was on Ulica Piekna Street, and a tall dark-haired unkempt Ukrainian walked up to someone who was brought into our ghetto from a nearby area. The Jew tried to move quickly to the other side of the cobbled street, but the Ukrainian demanded that he come back and stand in front of him. The giant Ukrainian figure started to call out vile names and made the Jew kneel before him. Then he stuck his bayonet in the man's stomach and walked away. To them we are not people ... we are just "units" or something that are to be disposed of like the trash.

Surdik, the Commander of the Ghetto and Jewish police, is rumored to use a Polish man to spy on the Jews in our ghetto. People say that this man, a chimney sweep, goes into people's houses to look at their stoves and scopes out if they have valuable items or any things that might have been gained from the black market. Then the Pole reports this to Surdik and the information is given to the Gestapo officials. All of us are afraid that we will be turned in for some minor mistake, whether we are guilty or not. We know that people are being sent away and never return.

Everywhere I look there is hunger. There is the atrocious stench of decomposing bodies and the pitiful moans of dying children. I hear desperate cries of people struggling for life against impossible odds. As always, I look down, and sometimes I have to walk around dead people. Eventually, a crew comes by and throws the dead people onto a wagon to be thrown into the mass grave. I constantly worry that I will be the next dead body to be thrown on the others to rot in the pile with other victims.

During the summer of 1942, my whole family is allowed to leave the ghetto and work on a nearby farm for one of our former customers who was a landowner in Sabnia, a local farm village. This farm owner has made special arrangements with the German Gestapo, and Jews are placed on a special detail list to do slave labor consisting of agricultural work. I think my parents made some special financial arrangement with someone so we could

A group of slave laborers at work. *(Memorial Book of Sokolow-Podlaski)*

leave the ghetto and be selected to work on this farm. Leaving the horrors of the ghetto was a "special privilege" and only the fortunate are placed on the list for slave labor in Sabnia.

During the day, the landowner rides on a large brown horse and makes certain that all the workers are staying busy and working hard. This arrangement is beneficial to both the farmer and my parents, since we are able to get food while working on the farm, and the landowner gets free labor. I guess that this landowner is then required to pay part of his profits or some sort of payment back to the Germans for use of this slave labor.

Another one of our customers from the butcher shop works on the farm as well, and he is a driver for the landowner. I enjoy having him on the farm because his wife, a warm-hearted loving woman, cooks huge dumplings for her family, and each one is filled with cherries or plums. She generously shares some of these with us. These special treats almost make me feel human and not like someone who is hated for being a Jew.

While my parents work, we are allowed to stay in a big barn. These times are pleasing to me because I am allowed to roam the farm during the day with my sisters. Days are happier for all of us because we are able to escape the ghetto and all the horrors and starvation that are present every day within the gates. Compared to ghetto life, these days are wonderful.

Unfortunately, we are only able to live on the farm for a couple of months. In October, which is near the High Holidays (Jewish New Year), we are told that we need to return to the ghetto. The Germans write an order for our return, and it was mandated that we all return with no exceptions. It is quite strange, but somehow my mother has made arrangements for Irene to stay. My mother tells me that the rest of the family will return to the ghetto together the following day.

I am really confused and keep asking why Irene is not coming with us, especially since it was nearing the High Holidays. My parents tell me that Irene is going to remain at the home of Hypolit and Francesca Gorski, who also live in Sokolow, about two blocks from the ghetto. I remember Mrs. Gorski from our old butcher shop because she would always buy lots of sausages and some sides of beef, and then talk to my mother for a long time. I always noticed they seemed to have some sort of relationship, perhaps not a friendship, but they seemed to enjoy talking about things and smiled and laughed.

I am really sad that Irene is allowed to live away from the ghetto, and I am forced to go back to that terrifying place. Once again the fear of death and the pain that comes with dying fills my mind. I am angry and jealous that Irene can stay with the Gorskis and have a life that is almost bearable and safe.

My fears are real, for on October 10, 1942, my world, as I know it ends, as does my life with my family. While we sleep, the German Gestapo, the Polish police and Ukrainian soldiers encircle the ghetto walls to begin the final liquidation of Sokolow. All Jews living in the ghettos in our area are to be rounded up and then sent to Treblinka for extermination.

Where is G-d?

I have learned two lessons in my life: first, there are no sufficient literary, psychological, or historical answers to human tragedy, only moral ones. Second, just as despair can come to one another only from other human beings, hope, too, can be given to one only by other human beings.

Elie Wiesel

Part Two:
The Hiding Place

Chapter 7
Where is G-d?

I stand in front of the massive student assembly in the suburban Chicago high school auditorium. Silent, I feel uncomfortable near the stage as I watch 1,200 high school juniors and seniors take their seats in this enormous facility. Many students smile and laugh as they enter. The group soon quiets as I near the podium to be introduced by the principal. I look into the eyes of a young boy who sits in the front row. He looks somewhat like me when I was his age, but I don't see the terror in his eyes that always filled my being.

I know speaking about my experiences will be very emotionally draining and difficult, because today is the memorial day of the liquidation of Sokolow. This day of the liquidation was the last time I saw my father and my precious baby sister Sara Rivka. I try to breathe deeply and concentrate, hoping this will create some inner balance. I must insure that each and every student learns about the evils of prejudice and hatred and the atrocities of what we call the Shoah or Holocaust.

I start to speak, but my heart still pounds, and my head ruminates about all the events that happened that terrifying morning in 1942 when we were violently forced from our hiding place. I try to rid my mind of the thoughts, but it is almost as if I were there once again. My body is present in this large auditorium, but my mind and my soul had returned to Sokolow, where I can see the Gestapo guard's machine gun, and I try to become invisible.

I can see my little sister Sara holding tightly onto my father's leg. I can hear the screams, and I can feel the tension in the Market Place as everyone pleads for their life. As I stand motionless in front of my audience today, I can almost taste death.

Holding on to the podium, I close my eyes for a moment. I tell the students they have the power to change the world and end the evil and hatred that have become commonplace in our lives. The words from the Talmud run through my mind, "To save one life is as if you saved the world." But I could not save my precious baby sister.

Fear! The fear of death and the impending pain of dying are terrifying. My teeth chatter, and my body convulses in tremors. I look up. It's October 10, 1942, and the sun is shining while these horrors occur. I have no tears, just uncontrollable shaking. Will death be very painful?

Everyone from the hiding place has been gathered together. The Ukrainians, the police and the Gestapo rejoice as we are driven in fear against our will. We are forced to sit in a circle in the ghetto Market Place. I try to move closer to my father as Sara hides under his arms. I wish someone would console my fears.

Sara cries, and the guards bark their orders and prod those who do not follow by beating them with large black clubs. I glance over at my baby sister, and she is holding a parcel of dried food wrapped in a handkerchief given to her by our mother. Wearing her beige stockings and short dark coat, she whimpers as she grasps her food.

Tears fill her eyes, and I see the terror and panic on her face. Sara's face has such a *haunting* look. She looks at me as if I could do something … anything. I'll *never* be able to erase that image from my mind. But, I am frozen and petrified. I don't want to die.

Everywhere I look in the Market Place, people are screaming. Over to my left within the circle area, I see an older woman sitting with blood running out of her stomach. I see other dead bodies, and there is a stench in the air. Perhaps the stench is the smell of fear … or is it the smell of death? I pray to G-d and ask Him to save me. But why would He save me when other children have been better behaved? Why would He save me when other children are more pious and have adhered to the Ten Commandments more fully than I? Please, I am consumed with the desire to live. Please G-d, let me live! Please, I need your mercy and your protection, and I promise I will pray and revere you forever.

Lackeys roam the streets of the ghetto searching for any remaining Jews who might be hiding. Men and women are being separated, and my mother has already been taken from us, but I don't know where. Guards march back and forth cursing at us, calling us dirty scum and filthy Jews. People are chased down the small hill from Rogofska Street to the back of our house. I keep looking around, but where is my mother?

A woman escapes from the ghetto, and two Poles violently drag her back to the Market Place as she fights for her life. Though trying to cover my face, I watch as the woman attempts resistance, grabbing at the ground as she kicks and punches the Poles in vain. The female victim is turned over to the Gestapo guard who has been holding the machine gun pointed at all of us. Standing in his black boots and dark uniform, he grabs the woman by her dark hair and tells her she must chose if she wants to be shot or be sent to Treblinka. The woman falls to the ground and begs for her life. The guard's head tilts back and with a loud bellowing laugh, he tells the woman she has taken too long to make the decision. He pushes the woman away by kicking her and shoots her in the head. As this happens, the Market Place is filled with screams as the Ukrainian lackeys and the Gestapo guard laugh.

All I feel is total despair. These monsters have the ultimate power over our destiny. They stand there laughing as many in the Market Place beg for their lives. I am overwhelmed with such hopeless, tragic fear. I pray if we must die, then let these murdering bastards die with us. Please G-d, allow me the pleasure of watching these savage demons die an excruciating painful death.

My father quietly bends over and whispers in my ear. I feel his trembling hand on my shoulder. He tells me I must try to escape. He tells me I must try to run and find my way to where my sister Irene has been hidden. I feel paralyzed. How can I escape? They will see me! My father looks at me with a look that denotes a stern order, and also one that displays the wish of a dying man. I know I must do as he says, but will they witness my escape and shoot me in the back as I attempt to run?

I slowly move to my knees and cautiously bend down and try to move behind the line of my neighbors who are sitting and facing the guard holding the automatic weapon. Keep low … keep low. I move to the cold damp ground and crawl ever so slowly behind those who are screaming and crying before me.

The Highway to Death: Treblinka. *(Photo courtesy Yad Vashem Film and Photo Archive)*

I Still See Her Haunting Eyes

58 Inch by inch I attempt to become part of the landscape and not be seen by the evil devils that desire our end. I feel coldness and sweat on my body, which also feels numb and hard. I must not be breathing, and all I see is the ground before me. I try not to hear the screams and try to block out the constant messages of fear that fill my brain.

Slowly I move along the line, crawling behind each person where the Market Place ends and the sewer runs along the street. Coaxing my body to move downward, I slither into the sewer ever so carefully. The sewer is filled with a muddy water mix, but all I know is I must find my way along it to exit the ghetto. It seems like the journey through the muddy sewer lasts forever. Time has stopped, and my heart pounds so loudly I'm sure the guard will hear it beating out of control.

Will they see me? Will they shoot me? Perhaps I will not feel the pain? Finally, somehow I find the strength to stand and run. Each step feels like I will never be able to take the next, and I feel weakened by the fear that is overcoming me.

Running along desolate streets, I continue my escape, but to my surprise I see no one. How is this possible? Perhaps everyone has already been brought to the Market Place, and I am the only one who has survived? I want to live! I don't want to die!

No one shoots at me! I don't understand why! Perhaps there is too much going on for them to notice me. The monsters must have seen me … but I most certainly do not deserve such good fortune.

So I run until I reach the small house that belongs to my Uncle Abram. His backyard meets the barbed wire at the edge of the ghetto that has become our inferno of hell. I know there is a hiding place under the kitchen floor, cleverly designed with a carpet that covers the opening. The carpet moves by strings so that it can be pulled to cover the entrance once you were safe within. It's almost as if the secret location isn't there at all when the carpet is in place. I run quickly into the cellar and close the secret door and maneuver the carpet.

To my astonishment, my aunt and my little cousin Hannah are kneeling quietly in the corner. Shaking, my aunt holds her young daughter tightly to her chest. Trembling, I sit in another dark corner of the cellar and place my arms around my knees. I try to comfort myself by rocking, but all I can do is cry. I sob and rock on the cold dirt floor of this damp cellar.

All I can see is Sara's face. She *haunts* me as I rock back and forth. How could I have left my family? Where was my mother? Why did my father tell me to leave? What will become of my father and little Sara? Will they be placed on cattle cars and sent to a death camp to be exterminated in the gas chambers? Will Sara be taken from my father and be alone in the cattle car, trampled by those who will not care for her? She is only a baby, and who will care for her?

As I rock, I feel nothing except the chilly dampness on my bottom and the cold sweat that envelops my body. I think back to the moment when my father told me to run away. Why did he say I should run to where Irene was being hidden? Until this moment, I did not realize that Irene had not returned with us because she was being "hidden."

Had my mother and father arranged all this before we had left the labor force on the farm? Had my parents known what would be our fate? Why was Irene chosen and Sara and I returned to the ghetto? My mind would not quiet, but somehow I fall asleep for a few hours holding my knees tightly to my chest.

חורבן

In Hebrew, the printing at the top translates as destruction. Prisoners wait to be executed. *(Memorial Book of Sokolow-Podlaski)*

Chapter 8
My Mother

I awake, still holding my knees against my chest. My body feels damp from the combination of the dirt floor and my own perspiration. Slowly and cautiously, I move out from beneath my protective area. Standing there, I hear no sounds at all. Perhaps everyone was dead? Had everyone left the ghetto, and my aunt, cousin and I were all alone?

Moving carefully towards the stairway in the cellar, I listen for sounds of danger. Hearing nothing I open the wooden door that was covered by the moving carpet. Seeing no harm, I climb out of the cellar and survey Uncle Abram's home. Nothing had changed since I had arrived, except the stifling silence.

I motion to my aunt and cousin Hannah that it appears safe to exit the hiding space. They reluctantly peer out, but my aunt refuses to leave. I plead with her, reminding her that the Germans would be back to liquidate all those remaining. She's frozen at the bottom of the stairs. Without much thought, my instincts tell me that I cannot stay here with them. I know this would mean certain death. I follow my inner voice and leave them alone in the cellar.

Leaving my only known remaining family, I inch my way out towards the kitchen door. Opening the door slowly, I walk toward the edge of the house and move towards the barbed wire fence that imprisons all who are Jews. I stand near the edge of a battered old oak tree and look around for guards. Miraculously, no soldiers are present, and the entire ghetto is quiet and abandoned.

Suddenly, I see a small woman along the barbed wire fence outside of the ghetto. For some unknown reason, I'm not fearful, and I stand there almost as if I have not witnessed the horrors just hours before. As I watch the elderly woman in her brown long skirt and scarfed head, she motions for me to come forward. She begins to yell at me in Polish, *"Chodz, chodz"* (Come, come). She appears insistent, and I instinctively run towards her surveying the vicinity for the Gestapo or Ukrainian guards.

She kneels and tries to help pull up the thorny strands of wire that are part of the barbed wire ghetto wall. She watches, almost as if she was my companion, for any sign of threat as I lay on my stomach and attempt to crawl through the sharp edged wires. As I squeeze through the narrow opening, my leg just below my knee catches part of the razor sharp wires. I can see a cut, which is very deep and about three inches long, but I continue to move through the barbed wire. At that moment my fear is greater than the blood and the pain, and I pull myself over to the ground outside our prison ghetto. The woman smiles at me and moves her hand, as if to tell me to run for safety. I begin to run and never look back.

Even as my leg bleeds, I run down Ulica Piekna Street and turn at the corner into the field that leads to the local farm village called Sabnia, just a short distance away. Running through the field, I keep moving forward, but bend down to assure myself that no one will see me. Thrashing through the field, I continue far enough from the road, so that I will not be seen by any motor vehicle that might carry German soldiers searching for more Jewish victims.

Noticing a truck in the distance, I drop to the ground and lay as flat as possible on the wild grasses that graced the field. I could feel the damp weeds on my bare legs. My short pants are stained with my own fresh blood, and my beige coat is torn and covered in mud. Remaining silent, I try to not move, and not even take a breath for fear of capture. Within moments the truck passes down the road and does not give the slightest indication that I have been noticed. I lay there for a while just to ensure my safety.

I continue to walk through the open fields dropping onto my stomach every time I hear the slightest noise from a passing vehicle. Lying on the ground, I sense my fear and growing desperation. How will I survive alone? When will the demonic monsters find me, and what would be my final moments before extermination?

That night, I approach the back door of a neighboring restaurant. The owner of the food establishment was a customer of ours, and someone who had been kind to us. Thinking the woman might help, I knock at the kitchen door innocently. A young man who works in the restaurant opens the door as I ask to see the owner. As the young worker walks to the front of the restaurant, I can see tables full of German soldiers and some Polish women sitting and eating.

Terrified, I am paralyzed as the young man taps me on the shoulder and hands me a loaf of round bread. He says the owner, Mrs. Kucewiczowi, cannot see me, and that I must leave immediately before I am captured. The young man pushes me a little, telling me again that I must go. I stare at him with such fear that he whispers that he will help me after he finishes with work. I hide behind the store, next to the wooden boxes that surround the kitchen doors, waiting for him.

Sitting there I began to feel very nervous. What if this young man turns me over to the Germans? Why would he try to save me? What would cause him to put his life in danger for a stranger? Clutching my precious bread close to my body, I run once again into the field towards Sabnia. Exhausted and unable to take one more step, I lay down in a small forest area near the field. I put the bread down on the ground as a pillow and immediately fall asleep.

When I awake in the morning, somehow I make my way to Sabnia. How could I have arrived here without being captured? As I near the village, I see some Jewish survivors also hiding in the fields. These few souls are others who escaped the same liquidation in Sokolow. Sharing our stories, two women tell me that my mother had survived the liquidation and that she was one of about four dozen people chosen to work as part of a labor group. One woman says they will pack and sort all the belongings that were left behind by the Jews. My mother and the other laborers would remain in the ghetto to do work for the German SS, selecting valuable items to be sent to Germany.

If my mother is still alive, I *must* go back to the ghetto. Immediately I begin to run back to find her. Along the way I see a Pole who was a friendly customer and frequented our butcher shop years ago. This Pole befriended us when we worked on the farm weeks ago, allowing my parents a place to stay while we worked on the farm. Scared and frightened, he tells me he could not hide me, but he offers me some food to sustain my journey.

I make my way back to the ghetto in hopes of finding my mother. Always watching for the murderers, I sneak back into the ghetto that is now virtually abandoned. There are no Germans, no Polish police, no Ukrainians, and no sign of the monsters that find pleasure in our elimination. The bodies of the dead have been taken from the Market Place and placed in the massive pit by our abandoned home.

Carefully, I hide behind buildings to make sure there are no guards. Hearing voices, I crawl on my stomach into the alley and hide to make sure I will not be caught.

Piles of belongings left behind by liquidated Jews through-out Poland. *(Photo courtesy United States Holocaust Memorial Museum)*

I Still See Her Haunting Eyes

I creep towards a warehouse filled with valuables, which once belonged to our people before the liquidation. Then I see about a dozen women sorting clothes and items that were left behind. There are no guards, only silence that is deafening. Then I see her. I run to my mother and throw my arms around her, unwilling to let go of my hold.

My mother comforts me, and tells me that I must hide, and that she will find some food and stay with me after sunset. It was difficult to leave her side, but I know she is part of a work force spared to gather, pack, and load the train filled with Jewish possessions to be sent to the Nazis. Besides, a guard will return soon to check on their work.

Obeying my mother's orders, I hide in one of the abandoned houses that are located near the Market Place. Immediately after dusk, my mother comes into my hiding place and shares a small portion of food she was able to find. I feel a sense of safety that I had not felt in the last week. What had become of my father? Of my sister? My mother tells me that she is unsure of their destiny because she had been pulled into a detail work location during the liquidation. We hug each other and cry quietly, soothing each other in the silence of the abandoned house.

Our time together only lasts for a few days as it becomes obvious that the work detail would soon come to an end. It was certain that everyone would be killed when the few remaining valuables were loaded onto the train. Once again with amazing insight, my mother told me that we must escape the ghetto before the Germans came back to exterminate the four dozen workers in the detail. It was certain that the Germans would have no need for them once the work had been completed.

On that very night, we find our way out of the ghetto just as the Gestapo is pulling up to the workstation. To my surprise, we do not escape alone. The German Jew, who had lived near our home, is also part of the work detail and leaving with us. Gedala, who had terrorized me so many nights with his predictions of our extermination, is now a partner in our escape into the fields. He's not my father, so why is he leaving with us? Why is he looking at her that way? Doesn't my mother know that this man scares me?

The moon is very bright on this late night. The cold air makes my body shiver. I'm forced to stand next to the man that I fear and dislike. He looks at me with indifference and anger. I am in the way. My being here seems to threaten their ability to find safety.

During the daytime, we hide in the forests, and by night we sneak out and ask farmers for portions of food. Sometimes we are lucky, and the Poles offer us some food or a safe haven for the night in their barn. One night we are able to stay in a stranger's barn on the warm hay, and the farmer's wife brings us cooked milk with potato inside. This gift of shelter and food is quite unexpected on this fall night.

Other times, the Poles chase us away and threaten they will turn us over to the Germans if we remain. Fugitives on the run, we are like animals being hunted on a safari, attempting to survive in a world filled with those who hate us.

Every day for nearly two weeks, we search for places of refuge. My mother pleads with a former neighbor, a farmer, to allow us to stay in hiding in his barn. She continues to attempt to convince the farmer to assist by giving us shelter and safety. My mother pleads and begs, and I see the terror on her face. The farmer beckons her, and she moves into the barn, out of sight with him. I hear nothing, and I'm worried standing alone next to Gedala, and fearful of what is happening inside the barn.

When my mother emerges from the barn, she approaches me and tells me I must go. She looks in my

I Still See Her Haunting Eyes

68 eyes and tells me I must leave them and find a place to stay. "Aaron, you must go and see if the Gorskis will take you in." Pulling a ring and a pair of earrings from her pocket, she tells me to give these to the Gorskis or anyone who will hide me.

My world is changing again, and my mother says I must leave her!

Chapter 9
Total Abandonment

How can I leave my mother? How can she tell me that she is staying with this evil man and that I must leave to find the Gorskis? I am only 10 years old, and she wants me to be on my own? Tears flow down my face like rain. My heart is broken, and the ache inside me is so deep it feels like I am bleeding. All I can feel is despair and sadness.

I look up at her in disbelief. How can she tell me to go away, to what will surely be my death? What if the Gorskis will not accept me? What if someone recognizes me as a Jew and turns me over to the Germans while I am making my way back to town?

Gedala moves towards my mother, and his eyes are red and stern. My mother does not move to embrace me; instead the man reaches over and shoves me away from my mother. Anger begins to boil inside me, but it is overtaken by the feelings of abandonment and despair.

Walking away, all I can do is cry. I will not look back. I will not give him the satisfaction of knowing that I am hurting. All I want to do is kill that man! He has taken my mother from me! But down deep, I also hate my mother for making me leave. I thought mothers are supposed to love and protect their children, and instead my mother chooses a strange man over me.

My steps become more like stomping on the dirt below. The frozen ground crunches beneath my feet, and I begin to run. Run … run … as fast as I can to try to escape from my sorrow. I run into the field and throw myself down on the ground and begin to beat the dirt with my fists. As hard as I am pounding, my tears pour out just as much. Everything within me feels like it is on fire. I have so much hatred inside me, and also so much despair and pain. How can all of those emotions be coming from within me at the very same time? I lay there crying and trembling. I don't know how long I remain on the ground, but I only remember waking a little later in the field.

I decide that I have to take care of myself. I can't trust or depend on anyone else. Despite my fear, there is this little voice inside me that says, "I'll show them. I won't die!" Continuing the pattern of hiding, I find places to hide in the woods at night, comforting myself with rocking and thinking of pleasant times with my sister Sara and playing soccer in my back yard. Whenever a painful feeling arises, I hit my leg repeatedly, firmly insisting that I will not allow myself to think about my mother and her abandonment.

During the day, I discover potatoes or sugar beets that had been hidden by farmers to keep them from freezing. I try to make the experience a game, imagining that I'm a wild animal trying to hide from my captors, finding food and discovering ways to outsmart my hunters. Each time I am successful in finding food or discovering a safe place to sleep, I feel as though I am strong and powerful.

One night, loneliness and despair overcomes me. My fantasy game that hides my pain no longer works. In desperation, I knock on a stranger's farmhouse door and plead with him to hide me. Outstretching my hand, I offer the jewelry my mother has given me if he will hide me. To my surprise, the man agrees to place me in the farmhouse cellar.

Within a short time, a young boy comes into the cellar and smiles as he greets me with hot soup and bread. I can't believe my eyes … this is the first hot food I have seen for probably a month! I'm overjoyed with hope and fantasize about being safe here in the cellar until the war's end.

But, the next morning the farmer slowly comes down the cellar steps. I watch his face as he nears me on the ground. He compassionately looks into my eyes and tells me that it's too risky for them to hide me. He puts his hand on my shoulder and tells me that he wants to help, but he can't risk being discovered by the Nazis, who would most surely kill them for hiding a Jew. The risk is too great.

He reaches into his pocket and hands me the earrings and the ring I had given him the night before. Once again touching my shoulder, the middle-aged man suggests that I give myself up to the authorities. Sadly, he says, "There is no longer any future for people like you!"

Where will I go? What will I do? It's as if this last abandonment was more than I could handle. Somehow I walk in a trance through the fields. I must have walked in this stupor for hours, and when I awaken from my state, I realize I have walked back to Sokolow and am nearing the Ghetto.

Looking down, I realize only then that I have been walking through open frozen fields that are covered in snow. My feet are freezing, and suddenly each step that I take causes great pain. Each step closer to the ghetto wall becomes more difficult and painful, but I trudge forward.

In the distance I hear a barking dog as my feet struggle for freedom in the muddy snow. Entering the ghetto area I see the open gate. There is no one around. The streets are empty and dark, and a strange eerie feeling fills the air. The ghetto is completely dark, and it's almost as if it's only inhabited by ghosts. I'm suddenly terrified. Knowing nowhere else to go, I run into the first empty house and fall on the floor, comforting myself with rocking until I fall asleep.

A few hours later, I see the sun entering the broken window of the empty house. Rising, I immediately decide that I must go to the Gorskis today and beg for their assistance. Making my way through the snow once again, I find myself just feet away from the Gorskis door. Their house is only a few blocks from the ghetto, but on that day, those two blocks seem like two miles. My mind surges with fear. What if they refuse to take me in? What if they turn me over to the Germans? I don't want to die!

I knock on the door, and the familiar face of Mrs. Gorski opens the door cautiously. Looking down, she becomes very angry and insists that it is very dangerous for me to be here. She seems stern and condemning as she points her finger at me and tells me I must leave right now. I can't leave … I just can't! I start to plead and beg and tell her that my mother had insisted that I come to her. I open my hand and show her the jewelry that my mother had given me to offer as a reward for my safety.

Once again, Mrs. Gorski points her finger at me and tells me that Irene was no longer staying with them and that she wants me to leave immediately. Standing there paralyzed, I begin to cry uncontrollably. Perhaps because of my tears or appearing so sickly, Mrs. Gorski tells me that she will allow me to stay in their attic, but only for a few days. After that time, she insists, I must leave and try once again to find my mother and stay in her care.

With that, Mrs. Gorski opens the door, and I slip quietly into the hallway and move towards the steps that lead to the attic.

Chapter 10
The Attic

Ever so carefully, I follow the woman up the stairs. She is angry that I'm here, but I follow her as her long skirt drags on the floor and catches each step as she walks. As I near the top of the stairs, a man stands on the landing. I look up sheepishly, and I see that it's Hypolit Gorski.

He is a large man, wearing a brownish black jacket and brown heavy pants. He looks at his wife, and they talk. His tone is very stern and condemning, and he never looks in my direction. Standing at the top of the stairs, he tells Mrs. Gorski he is going to church, and he goes down the stairway without giving me the slightest glance. I turn and watch him descend the stairs, thankful that he has not declared that I must leave. I feel a sense of hope and tremendous relief.

On the landing, I see a small wooden door that leads to an attic. I watch Mrs. Gorski open the creaking door, and inside I see only darkness and the starkness of the wooden walls against the tin roof. Mrs. Gorski tells me to go in and instructs me to stay in this same spot until she returns. Obediently, I follow her instructions.

Within a few moments she returns from the hallway and hands me an old dirty wooden pail. She tells me to use this pail as my toilet. She goes to the far end of the little attic and grabs some straw and places it in a torn brown burlap bag. She points to the corner of the dark attic and tells me to form a bed with this straw where the roof and floor meet.

Whispering to me, she informs me that she thinks this

location will be safe, but warns that I must remain in the attic and that I must be absolutely silent or someone might learn of my existence. Until that moment, I hadn't even realized that this house also had other tenants. I had been so thankful to climb the stairs to the attic that I was unaware that the Gorskis lived in the upstairs apartment and others lived below in two small apartments.

With deep scorn on her face, Mrs. Gorski exits the room, and I am left alone in the dark and the cold. I move toward the bag of straw, spreading it into a little bed, snuggling into its contents with my knees against my chest, trying only to stay warm.

The room is very cold, and the floor of the attic is composed of dirt. I look up to the roof and cautiously touch the tin roof above me. The silvery tin roof is covered in white frost, which is freezing, and I quickly remove my hand. A small beam of sunlight shines through the separation in the tin roof, which becomes the only light that invades the darkness. Kneeling, I try to lie down on the straw and move it various ways to create a small bed.

The attic is cold and uninviting, but it is safety, and my dreams seem to be answered. I try again to pull my knees into my chest and rock to stay warm. Laying in silence, I think of my mother and wish she was here to comfort me. I think of every crease in her face and remember how she used to comfort me with warm blankets after our weekly bath.

Then I think of Gedala, and rage begins to grow in the pit of my stomach. Why has she chosen him over me? Is she in love with this man? How could she want to be with him instead of me? Slowly my eyes fill with tears, and I try to think of happier times as I rock myself to sleep.

A few rays of sunlight fill the tiny attic with a glimpse of day. Waking, I lay there in a fetal position. Then I realize that I had urinated on myself. Perhaps this had kept me warm during the night, but now the semi-frozen urine

Francesca and Hypolit Gorski

was caked on my clothes and body. I see the sunlight peeking through a crack in the tin roof. The light feels like a friendly stranger coming into the attic to comfort me. But the tin roof was covered with ice and frost that had formed on it during the night. As I try to move, I feel the intense cold and immediately huddle again to stay warm.

After a while Mrs. Gorski slowly opens the door and peers inside the attic. She walks towards me and hands me some soup and a small piece of bread, which I hide in my sock. The food is a welcome sight, but her tone and conversation is anything but welcoming. She reminds me that I am placing her and her family in tremendous danger and states that Irene no longer lives with them. She continues by telling me that she had made an arrangement with my mother to hide one child, not two.

"Your mother is a shrew, a Jew shrew who talked me into taking in your sister and jeopardizing my safety as well as my husband's. You two are a curse to me. This war is never going to be over. The Germans are going to conquer the whole world, and I'll never be rid of you."

I can only sit quietly and look down. There is nothing to say. I must accept her angry comments and be grateful for the chance to be safe in this attic. Mrs. Gorski tells me that she thought it would be possible to hide my sister Irene because she might pass for a Gentile, but I could not pass.

"What would be more recognizable than a male Jew? You put us all at risk … All they need to do is find you and have you drop your pants, and we all will be sent away to a death camp. Damn your Jew mother for sending you to us!"

That day I sit on the straw and think about all the things that Mrs. Gorski had said. I keep wondering if there is some other place that I could run, but I know this was my only chance for survival, and I desperately want to live. I keep thinking of better days.

My mind sweeps to the time my father had gone to the dentist to have his tooth removed. Because of his intense pain, he did not go back to the butcher shop, and instead came home to a house that was empty except for me. Spending the day together, we cooked eggs on the stove and enjoyed our scrambled eggs like they were a majestic meal made just for a king. This is one of the few times that I remembered spending so much time with my father and the laughter we shared. The memory brings a smile to my face, and I huddle on my straw bed rocking myself to sleep.

The next morning Mrs. Gorski comes into the attic and empties the pail that I used for my toilet. Once again she informs me I am a burden and that they had little to eat as it was because of the strict rationing imposed by the Germans. Sternly she reminds me that I'm creating a more dangerous situation for all of them, and that is why everyone wants me to leave. She says that I am putting everyone at risk, including my sister Irene.

What did she say? Did that mean that my sister Irene is still alive and living with them? Had she lied to me, that Irene was living in the same building? I quickly ask if my sister is still living with them, and she says nothing. She looks at me with coldness in her eyes and then moves towards the door. She looks back and tells me that she now cannot let me leave because she's afraid that if the Germans captured me, I would tell them where I had hidden.

As she closes the door, I hear her mumble terrible things to herself about my mother and why had she listened to her plan. Nothing more is said about Irene, and I'm sure I must have heard her wrong. Was Irene in this house or wasn't she? Is she still alive, or had she moved away from the Gorskis' house to another place of hiding?

That day I try to occupy myself by picking the lice out of my clothes. It was a nasty job, but it was somewhat stimulating and entertaining in some bizarre way. It does occupy my alone time, and each bug crunched between my finger and my nail is one less little menacing bug to bite me.

As night falls, the attic darkens, and I begin to think of poor Sara. What has happened to my baby sister? I keep seeing those eyes that *haunt* me. Where was she? Had she been taken away to the concentration camp? Was she all alone? Who had cared for her in the cattle car nearing Treblinka? Did Sara die alone with no one to wipe her tears or comfort her? Without a sound, I begin to cry and start rocking on my side on the straw. The tiny attic becomes colder and darker, and eventually I fall asleep shivering.

The next morning, to my surprise, the door opens, and Irene appears in the doorway to the attic. She looks the same as I remembered, but perhaps an inch or two taller. Her hair is pulled back, and she's dressed in dark dull clothing that seems to make her look older. Irene appears a little thin, but she smiles at me and comes near with a pail of hot water.

She speaks to me about what had happened since she arrived at the Gorskis as I try to wash up, but it's somewhat useless. I am so full of lice and other vermin that the hot water does little to remedy the problem. Irene continues to talk to me for a few more minutes and then says she must leave because she was ordered to only stay for a short while. She is fearful of being punished for staying too long and waves goodbye.

Irene starts to leave, stops and reminds me that our mother had placed her in hiding. "Now the Gorskis have to worry about hiding two of us." My eyes fill with tears as she exits the attic. I'm sad because she is leaving me alone, but at the same time I am elated that my sister is alive and living within this home. I look at her and then quickly down to the ground.

Once again I am alone in the attic realizing I am a burden and a threat to everyone. What else could I do but come here as my mother instructed?

Chapter 11
Loneliness is My Constant Companion

Most of my days hidden in the attic consist of thinking about food. My hunger becomes my major focus. I should be thankful that Mrs. Gorski brings me any leftover soup in the pot in which it was cooked. She also brings me a slice of bread, which I use to gather up every little drop of soup that might hug the sides of the large cooking utensil.

For some unknown reason, I seem to enjoy the soup when it has been sitting for a while untouched, becoming sour and jelled. Somehow, it almost makes the soup hearty in consistency, and the sourness makes my taste buds come alive, if only for a few moments. The most delightful part of my day is the time I have savoring my slice of bread and my miniscule portion of soup.

At night I find myself awakening from a dream sitting around our large wooden kitchen table at home in Sokolow. I see myself sitting with my family, and the table is covered with an abundance of all sorts of tasty treats. I see my mother, father and Sara smiling at me as we all play a game holding our forks ready to lunge at the gathered food.

I reach for my favorite treat on the table, which is warm, freshly baked bread. I can almost taste the first bite of black bread smeared with heavy butter and covered in sugar. The dream is always so wonderful, and then I awake with the hunger pains in my stomach.

I Still See Her Haunting Eyes

Rubbing my eyes upon awakening, I remember the dream. It isn't odd that I'm dreaming of my favorite childhood treat of bread, butter and sugar … but it's interesting that Irene was not sitting at the table in my dream. Perhaps she was somewhere else? Maybe I do not see her at the table because she had not come to visit me here in the attic for a while.

Alone … always alone. I yearn to see Irene, my mother or anyone who really cares about me. I want someone to comfort me and erase my despair and pain. Staying in the attic for what seemed a month or more, my only companions are the rays of sunlight, the lice on my body, and the mice that also try to stay warm in the winter.

As I sit up on my straw bed, my mind again focuses on my stomach that aches with hunger. I wonder what it would feel like to have a full stomach and not be hungry. What more could anyone want? I keep wondering if Irene is given more food, and then my heart sinks because it is sinful to not be grateful for what I have been given.

I want Irene to be safe, but part of me is jealous that she is allowed to stay in the warmth of the apartment and sleep in a bed. I am filled with envy, imagining that she is sitting at a table and allowed to eat food of her choice and able to talk to people whenever she likes. But, as soon as those enter my mind, I only feel guilty for thinking such selfish thoughts.

So I sit in silence. All the time I stay in my little corner, which has become my home. I fantasize about clean clothes without the lice that invade my pants and shirt. I dream of taking a hot bath and being wrapped in warm blankets by my mother. But in the next instant, my thoughts return to my hunger. The pain is intense, and the ache in my stomach is constant.

After weeks and weeks of hunger, I decide that I must do something different. How long can I endure this hunger and pain? There is a wooden trough outside of the Gorski's kitchen upon the landing. I can see this trough through the cracks in the wooden wall, and each day I see Mrs. Gorski throw all their food scraps inside the wooden container. As I watch this one morning, she fills the wooden trough with potatoes peelings, and other unwanted garbage pieces.

Occasionally, I see Mr. Gorski move to the trough and urinate on top of the contents and then walk back from the landing into the apartment. Each day these unwanted foodstuffs and unwanted garbage are mashed and chopped up, and then the chickens and livestock are fed from this trough. For so many days and nights I watch as the animals are given more sustenance than I am given in my ration of daily food.

Tonight my stomach aches more than ever before. I keep thinking of the scraps of food and imagining how much better my stomach would be if I could eat some of these scraps. I realize this is garbage, and it has been mixed with urine, but my hunger and desperation are becoming too great to have such things matter. In that moment I devise a plan. When the Gorskis go to sleep tonight, I will sneak out of the attic and find my way to the trough and its discarded treasures.

And so it was … as night fell, I wait. Very slowly and cautiously I open the door to the attic. It had been months since I had seen the landing outside of this doorway and had obediently followed the orders to remain quiet and captive in this hiding place. But today, I could do it no more. Being so quiet and careful, I crawl on my knees to the landing and then out to the trough.

Disregarding the dirty situation, I place my hands into the mixture and scoop out some potato peels and scraps of vegetables. Starved, I eat the scraps until I feel comfortable. I sit for a minute and notice that my stomach does not ache. From that moment on, I know this trough would be my savior when I can not endure the hunger pains. Yet, when I sneak back into my hiding place, my stomach begins to twist and turn and leaves me with diarrhea all night, and I know right away that I will not return to the trough.

So again in the attic, I sit in silence. All the time I stay in one corner and am always cold and hungry. I never get to take a bath, brush my teeth or cut my hair.

The winter is extremely painful between the freezing cold, my nagging hunger and the desolate solitude. Being alone in that dark and totally filthy place is almost too much to endure. My desperately lonely existence, the long freezing nights on the earth floor, and the worn sack of straw, infested with lice and fleas … It all forces such bitter tears from my heart. Why do I have to live in such fear? Why am I hated and destined to die in pain?

I look around, and I am so alone in this filth. The winter is now so severe that the frostbite on my skin makes me break out in sores. These infections itch, and I scratch the sores, causing bleeding and more pain. To add to my miserable condition, my straw is full of bugs, and I hate G-d for making me die in pain all alone. What had I done to deserve this fate? Why was I born a hated Jew?

As winter turns to spring, the less frigid temperatures became more bearable. For so many nights I had shivered myself to sleep, and now spring is a welcome guest. Each day I awake and move briskly in place, trying not to make any noise. This activity warms my body, and the blood flows throughout my system. Eventually, in late morning, after everyone had eaten breakfast, Mrs. Gorski enters the attic and brings me food that eases my hunger.

Days pass, but nothing ever changes. Each morning Mrs. Gorski enters the attic and walks only a few steps into my hiding place. She picks up the pail that is filled with my waste and replaces it with a similar old wooden pail. She looks down at me with contempt and mutters insults about my mother and her manipulation. She always reminds me that I am unwanted and tells me that I'm a burden to her and Mr. Gorski. Always she exits the room shuffling her feet on the dirt floor. She tells me that I am putting them at risk, and she would be hung in the village square if it's discovered that she's hiding Jews.

After so many months of ridicule and verbal abuse, I have learned to tune out Mrs. Gorski's words, because my focus is purely on the food that she holds in her hand. My thoughts are always on the food, and her utterings have no impact on me. I know that I'm unwanted, and I'm quite certain if there was a way for the Gorskis to rid themselves of me, I would be gone. I wish someone would hold me, nurture me, tell me that I was a good boy and that I had nothing to fear. I wish that my mother was here, or that my father would place his arm around me and promise me that everything would be okay.

But those dreams never come true. Each day is another day of isolation and loneliness. With the loneliness comes some hope now that the nights are less frigid. Spring might bring the end of the war, or perhaps some miracle that will end my despair.

With spring there is a surprising event ... thunderstorms. When the rain pounds down on the tin roof, the noise is deafening. Thunder adds to the camouflage, and during those times I run around the attic and even raise my voice and scream because no one can hear me.

On those days, the rain allows me a chance to be a little boy who needs to play and have fun. The rain comes down with such force and makes such thunderous noise against the tin plates that I am able to cry, even sing and let my pent-up emotions escape. I rejoice in having the opportunity to release my voice. Rain becomes my welcome friend, and life takes on somewhat of a hopeful tone on the days that the rain joins my existence.

I Still See Her Haunting Eyes

On other days, I find flies making their way into my hiding place. I catch the invaders and then pull off their wings for fun. I don't know what is more fun … the catching of the flies or the pulling off of their transparent wings. After a while I can even tell the boy flies from the girl flies from their anatomy, because the boys have something sticking out when I press on their stomach.

As I play with the flies captured in my hands, I try to imagine what it would be like to be able to fly. How miraculous it would be to be a fly and able to escape this land that hates me for being a Jew. Why do these people hate me so much? What horrible sin have I committed that brings me this type of destiny? At times I wish I was dead … but my overwhelming desire to be reunited with my family and live is much greater than my desire to die.

But, days later, my dream of survival returns. I imagine that I am the only survivor, and life is exciting. The world will welcome and embrace me. Ultimately, the dream fades, and the heat of the summer takes over. The sun bakes down on the tin plates of the roof, and the attic becomes an inferno.

The air feels like it is being sucked out of the attic. It is impossible to touch the roofing plates, because it is an absolute oven. The heat is so intense that I can barely breathe because the air feels thin and humid. I lay there, totally still, soaked in sweat. If I remain quiet and do not move, I find that I can stay a little cooler, and it's easier to breathe. If I can survive for one more hour … just one more hour and then the evening will come. The rats and mice move at will, and my attic mates have a greater potential for life than me.

During those quiet times, I somehow take myself outside of my body. By that I mean that I have learned how to take myself to some sort of different place in my mind. My body is in the attic, but my mind is far away dreaming of times when things were pleasant, or fantasizing about spending time with my parents and sisters. Unsure of how I have mastered this escape, I find that some days pass from dawn to dusk as if they happened in a few moments. When I'm able to put myself in this trance, nothing can hurt me, and I cannot feel the loneliness, the despair, the hunger or the hurt.

This daydreaming or trance of sorts is a great way to handle my loneliness. I imagine myself surviving this horrible atrocity and then becoming some sort of hero of the novel I create in my mind. I see myself being accepted by others and then showered with affection and praise because of my heroism. I imagine being an adult, wearing a cleanly laundered shirt and working in a business of my own. The sunlight enters my daydreams and becomes the beacon of promise, almost like a message from Heaven showering me with warmth and strength.

I'm not quite sure why certain days bring up vivid memories from my past. Perhaps it's the smell that fills the attic or something hidden that churns within me as I begin to remember times past. I remember how a young German had come to our house in Sokolow in 1939.

Standing tall with his blondish brown hair, his appearance was quite different than those in Sokolow. His face had few lines except for the dimples that appeared when he laughed during a conversation. I remember he wore a steel semi-circled plate on his chest with the inscription "*Gott ist mit Uns*" (G-d is with us). I was always staring at that silver plate whenever he came to our house to visit. I was never sure why he came to our house, or why he treated us like friends, but we believed that the Germans were enlightened people, and he seemed to enjoy being with us and talking to my mother.

How wrong we were! Who would have believed these same Germans would enter our country and attempt to exterminate all of the Jews as if we were rats. Who would have believed Germans, like this man, would come into our town and kill people for pleasure without the slightest remorse? Who would imagine a man like that German would round up my father, my aunts and uncle and my baby sister Sara and take them to their death in a place like Treblinka? Who would have imagined the atrocities that would fill our world with pain and despair?

Why was I born a Jew? Why did I deserve this destiny? Who had I harmed to have to endure this fate?

As I sit quietly in my hiding place, the living truth is obvious. The Germans intend to continue this war until all of us are dead. They will continue killing Jews until there are no more left on this earth. That only means that someday they will find me and my sister Irene, and we will become two more Jews recorded on their death roster.

Chapter 12
The Apples

I have spent almost nine months alone in my hiding place. Within that time period, I have only seen my sister Irene when she is allowed to enter my attic prison. When she is permitted to visit my safe place, she is only able to spend a few minutes in conversation with me.

It is hard to tell whether it is better to see her or whether it is worse. On one hand, seeing her is so wonderful, but then I feel the depression and despair at a deeper level when she is forced to leave. I want her to visit me, but I don't want to hurt so much when she leaves. I discover that I exist in some state of constant pain and depression, and feeling something hopeful opens me up to disappointment and increased feelings of emptiness.

Looking through the tin roofing, I spend many of my days dreaming of living outside this prison. It is nearing the fall months in 1943, and the leaves on the trees are beginning to drop, but not before Mr. Gorski gathers all the ripe apples that have been growing on two massive apple trees behind the house. Each day I watch him reach to grasp the red juicy prize, and my mouth fills with saliva from anticipation. He fills a large bucket with these treasures, and the next day he returns until the apples on the tree disappear.

As these cool fall days continue, I peer out the openings in the tin roof and see the remaining apples on the tree. In my fantasy, I am able to fly out of my prison and land on the branches and rest there, devouring the tasty apples until I can eat no more. The fantasy brings much happiness, and some moments I can almost taste the apple that I desire.

Near the end of fall, Mr. Gorski enters the attic. I tremble because Mr. Gorski has not come into the attic during my captivity. He looks at another corner of the attic and holds a large basket filled with apples in his arms. Ignoring my presence, he places the apples on the dirt floor and walks back to the landing. I sit there frozen, wondering if he is bringing me some of the juicy red apples that I have dreamt about the last few months.

Returning quickly to the attic he drags in a large burlap bag of freshly cut straw. Though he still doesn't talk to me, I remain in the same spot on the dirt floor watching his movements. I watch him create a little bed for the prized apples from the fall harvest. He places the straw on the floor in the corner, and then he lays out all of the juicy apples on top of the straw in neat straight rows. When he has finished creating the lines of apples upon the straw, he then takes the remaining straw and places it gently on top of them. He continues to place straw on the fruit until no color from the apples can be seen.

I sit there in amazement because the apples have more straw on them than I have available to keep me warm in this horrid attic prison! He obviously has prepared this bedding for the apples, attempting to preserve them in the cold of the attic. The straw is the comforting blanket to keep them safe from freezing. But, they are only apples, and I am an 11-year-old boy who will tremble and shiver in this freezing prison this winter.

Mr. Gorski then turns towards me and sternly tells me I must never eat even one of these apples. He points his finger at me and then raises his fist insisting that these apples are only for him and his wife. If I touch the apples, if he discovers that even a single apple is missing, it will prove beyond a doubt that I am not appreciative of the help that he and his wife have given to my sister and to me.

He strongly reminds me that helping two Jews has placed his family in great danger. He points his finger again at my face, and his eyes frighteningly convey the warning to not disobey his orders. With that, he turns and leaves me alone in the attic with the apples and my hunger.

I desperately want one of those apples, but I am strictly forbidden to touch them. How can you forbid someone from eating food when they are starving? How can anyone resist the temptation? I try to resist. I do appreciate the opportunity to stay alive in safety in this hiding place. But, I am so hungry, so very hungry, and those apples are a gift I desire above all else.

I spend days looking at the apples, and my starvation increases to the point of desperation. I try to talk myself out of taking even one apple, reminding myself that Mr. Gorski has warned me against such an act. I do not want to go against his orders since they have been kind to hide me in the attic, but my stomach aches. I feel like I'm going insane with this temptation so close. How can anyone resist?

I then create a plan. I will take one small apple from the rows of neatly placed apples and replace the straw, but not before I have changed the distance between the apples to make it appear like nothing has been altered. As I move the apples, I feel no guilt, only anticipation of placing the apple in my awaiting mouth. I patiently adjust the location of each apple in the lines so no one can detect the change.

When I complete this task, I take my prize to my straw bed and hold the red gift in my hands. Before I take a bite, I decide to rub the cover of the apple on my jacket. Over and over again I rub the coat of the apple making the color deeper in richness and more appealing. Finally I take a bite of the apple. I begin to feel a sense of pleasure, which pushes out any guilt I might hold.

I Still See Her Haunting Eyes

I know that I should not eat any more of these apples. I am certain that Mr. Gorksi will be furious with me if I steal any more apples. If he finds some missing, it will prove that I am not appreciative of the help he and his wife have given to my sister Irene and me. He will believe that I do not appreciate that he has placed his own family in terrible danger. I know for sure I will go to Hell. I am so evil ... I should not take what is not mine.

Even with the knowledge that I am betraying his orders, I seem to not be able to control my desire for the tempting apples. So on the next day, I steal another apple and try once again to hide the fact that it is missing. As the days go on, I become more inventive in my terrible crime of stealing the treasured crop. While Mr. Gorski is at church praying for his entry into Heaven, I move all the apples and one by one I rearrange them taking my prized possession from the till. I arrange and re-arrange them leaving no space between the jeweled commodities. And so, as the separation between the apples becomes greater, my crime is soon discovered!

The fateful day is in December. Mr. Gorski enters my attic and moves towards the prized apples. At first I believe he will not notice the changes I have made in his bed of prized apples. I watch as he stands over the apples uncovering them slowly and cautiously. Then I see the tension in his neck as he moves his shoulder up towards his head. I am able to catch sight of his face, which is becoming red like the treasured apples.

Without warning, he stands over me as he holds his fist near my face and screams at me. He calls me every ugly name that he knows, and reminds me over and over that he and his wife are good people. He tells me that if it was not for him, I would not be alive. I know he is right, but how can he understand what it is like living in this prison attic starving? How would he be able to resist if he was faced with the same situation?

I try to apologize and look down as I keep saying over and over that I am sorry. Mr. Gorski continues to call me names. I retreat into my straw bed and pull my knees into my chest and begin rocking. Mr. Gorski walks to the attic door and slams it, but not before he calls me a dirty Jew.

Early the next morning, Mr. Gorski enters the attic and removes all the apples. I stay on my straw bed, and he only focuses on the apples as he begins to fill a wooden bucket with the precious treasures. The straw is pushed aside, and it is easy to see that he is still filled with anger and rage as he collects the fruit. I watch every apple as it is placed in the large wooden container, finding myself counting as they are piled upon each other.

When Mr. Gorski has finished, he turns and stares at me and tells me that I am not trustworthy and that I am not appreciative of his kindness. I look down, hoping to be invisible, but I feel guilty and shameful for my actions and my hunger.

Fall turns into the winter of 1944 and once again the bitter cold becomes my attic companion. I had forgotten the cold's powerful effect on my physical body and my emotions. I am so tired of being captive in this place with my constant hunger, the lice, filth and my loneliness.

The passing of winter is a blur. Each day I shiver, tremble and focus on survival. Most of my days, I am in the trance state that keeps me safe from the weather and reality. I awaken … I eat my daily portion of food … I fight to stay alive … and then I fall asleep.

One day I am so bored that I decide to draw designs on the dirt floor with my urine. I become an artist with my own elimination being the paint. I begin to find this a pleasing activity, which allows me to have some fun in a morbid fashion. As I pee, I create beautiful designs on the earth floor. I have no audience, but I'm sure these masterpieces are some of the best artistic endeavors ever created. So each day, this activity becomes part of my daily routine.

Enjoying my artistic creation one early morning, I smile at my palette on the dirt floor until Mr. Gorski enters the attic. He screams at me and tells me that my urine has seeped along the ceiling floor and dripped on his head as he walked down the stairs. He calls me names and tells me that I am a filthy Jewish pig. The horrid verbal abuse continues as I look down and feel only shame as I am yelled at. I try to hide and make myself invisible.

I try to imagine that this all will be over soon and that I will see my father and mother and my sisters once again. Yes, I imagine that we will all be together again and then I am no longer scared. I am no longer cold. I am no longer hungry. I am no longer alone. The dreams fill my soul with warmth as the days pass.

The spring of 1944 comes, and I realize that I have lived in this attic for more than a year and a half. How is that possible? How have I survived? Why is G-d making me suffer? Will this ever end?

Chapter 13
1944 Brings
the Strawberry Girl

I accept loneliness as part of my fate. My days seem to pass much easier than the nights. The freezing cold, the darkness, the isolation, and the filth are much more difficult to endure. The nightmares always come, and I awake just at the instant that I am being killed.

My tormented dreams are so frightening that I am unable to go back to sleep, and instead I tremble and think about painful means of dying. When I awake, I discover I have wet myself again. I'm sure if I allow myself to give in to my fatigue, I will return to my horrific dream and once again I will be forced to watch my own impending death.

It is now the early months of 1944, and I am thankful that Irene comes to visit me more often. I'm not quite sure why the Gorskis are letting her join me in my attic more often, but I have something positive to anticipate. I am grateful for each moment we have together.

As we talk, Irene tells me about some of the other tenants in the apartment building and what she knows about each and every one. She tells me there is a young woman, perhaps in her 20s, who lives in the apartment with them. She rents a bedroom from Mrs. Gorski, and Irene mends her stockings and washes her clothes.

The college student has a boyfriend who is a professor. Riding his bicycle to see the young woman each weekend, the suitor stays in the apartment, which is on the other side of a portion my attic wall. I listen to Irene tell me about the couple, but I choose not to tell her that I have heard the two of them through the wall engaging in something that sounds sexual. As a 12-year-old boy, I am very interested in hearing everything I can about the couple and visualize what they do behind the wall.

Irene says she overhead Mrs. Gorski say that the young professor works for the *Armia Krajova* (the underground Polish home army). Whenever the young man comes to visit, Irene must leave the apartment and join me in the attic. I ask her if she thinks they know about me, and she says she is unsure, but doubts that they have any idea of my presence.

There is a couple who live in one of the apartments downstairs, but Irene says she knows little about them, but that they have a young daughter, a preschooler. Irene thinks that the father is a teacher but is unsure if that is accurate. My sister goes on to say she has never ventured outside of the Gorski's apartment, and there is another couple in the remaining downstairs apartment that she has never seen.

My hopes now center on waiting for spring and occasional visits from Irene. As the winter fades and the rays of the sun warm my prison home, I feel more optimistic. All I want is to live and to be freed from this attic to run in the yard that I see through the tin roof.

One morning I peer through the roof and see a young girl playing in the backyard. The blonde-haired girl must be around five or six, because she looks about the same size as my sister Sara. The little girl looks so happy playing and romping, and immediately I think of my baby sister who was sent to die in Treblinka.

I want to cry, but there are no tears left inside. I want to play outside and kick a soccer ball, throw stones at a target, or just run and jump, feeling the crisp air against my face. Why should I be locked in this prison? Why must I pick lice off my clothes and ache from hunger while she is allowed to play? But I realize that I will never be able to have that pleasure of being normal.

In total boredom, I often pry open the separations in the tin roofing plates to observe the back yard. One day I again focus on the little girl.

I stand intently as she plays, watching her every move. I see her holding a small bowl and eating ripe strawberries. She begins to walk back and forth, holding each strawberry in her little hand. My eyes become larger as I strain to watch as she nibbles small bites off the strawberry and skips. My heart breaks from pain and envy. Down on the ground a little girl is eating strawberries, and life seems so normal. I'm up here hiding to save my life, and if I were not Jewish, my life would be like hers.

I want to be like her. I would gladly renounce my religion and do anything to be normal. I yearn to be anything but a Jew! I'm sure my thought of renouncing my religion and my G-d will insure my place in Hell, but I wish I did not have to endure this pain any longer. Why was I born a Jew?

Feeling so depressed, I leave the tin roof opening and fall on my straw bed and begin to rock. Trying to think of happy memories, I focus on Irene and her most recent visit. I remember Sokolow and the hill that came down from Ulica Rogofska Street to Ulica Piekna Street. We would take our sled on snowy days and spend the entire time sledding. As a small smile fills my face, I remember the old woman who sold hot *bubliczky* (potato latkes) at the bottom of the hill. We would give her a ride down the hill in trade for a warm, tasty *bubliczky*.

I think about my mother hugging me, the times she would pinch my cheek, twisting it until I thought I would burst. She always teased me in that way, and the thought makes my pain go away as I rock myself into a trance.

From time to time I go stir crazy with boredom and hunger and the need to do something … anything. I move around in the attic, and one day, the Strawberry Girl thinks there is someone up in the attic. She's convinced someone is up there. Irene tells me that Mrs. Gorski told her about the Strawberry Girl and her questions. She says that the girl's father says it's just rats running around in the attic, but the little girl is not willing to believe this story. Irene makes sure that I know, in hopes that I will stay quiet and make less noise.

But one day I hear people coming up the stairs to the attic. The creaky door to my attic suddenly opens. Hearing the noise, I run swiftly to the corner of the attic where my bed meets the roof. I try to squeeze into the corner hidden by the darkness of the surrounding boards that hover around me. As quickly as it opens, the door closes and all I see are two heads peer in for a moment and then a man said, "See, there is no one there!" With that they were gone.

Irene tells me a few days later that the invaders were the Strawberry Girl and her father. Mrs. Gorski had told Irene that the little girl insisted someone was upstairs, and that her father took her into the attic to prove she was mistaken. I tell Irene that I'm sure that the father did catch a glimpse of me, but acted as if he saw nothing. Of course, when Mrs. Gorski comes the next morning to give me my allotted ration of food, she scolds me for being loud. "You are a nasty boy and putting us in danger. You are a little bastard, and you live to make me miserable. You must be quiet, or we will all be found and killed!"

I don't think I know how to cry anymore. The tears are locked inside and mingled with sorrow, grief and hatred. The thoughts of revenge are always present. I wish I could be the one to capture Hitler and cut into him with razor blades. I would then rejoice as I pour salt into his wounds. I wouldn't allow him to die … I'd like to watch him suffer like he has made me suffer. I want to torture him and his killers for all the pain and death he has inflicted on my family.

Hate keeps me from surrendering to my pain, and it makes sure that I never give up.

Chapter 14
Welcoming the
Thundering Skies

It is the summer of 1944, and the German army is in full retreat as the Red Army launches its summer offensive. I hear from Irene that things are going very badly for the Nazi regime, and the Russians are nearing as we pray for the end of the war.

Irene visits me often in the attic and warns that I must be very quiet. It seems that the Gestapo has ordered the eviction of the occupants of our building. Mrs. Gorski was able to maintain her housing, promising to do the laundry and cook for the German soldiers who have moved into the two downstairs apartments.

My sister reports she doesn't know what happened to the Strawberry Girl's family or the other occupants in the building, but that she and the Gorskis have been allowed to stay as long as they maintain the daily household duties for the Nazi occupants. Everyone is terrified in the Gorski household.

It is almost impossible to believe that I am hiding in an attic above soldiers who want me dead! Most of my day I live in terror because one wrong sound might bring the German soldiers upstairs to my place of safety. I remain sitting on my straw bed most of the time and dream about being free.

The Germans soldiers inhabit the downstairs apartment for about four weeks. Irene reports that one of the soldiers was drunk one night and began walking up the stairway toward the attic. Luckily, Mrs. Gorski heard the ruckus and was able to encourage him to go downstairs by holding his arm and talking to him as she quickly led him back to his apartment.

On the fourth week of the German soldiers' stay, the Russian Army was nearing our town. The Germans soldiers are retreating, and the Russian Air Force begins to bomb and strafe our town. Since we have a Gendarme station and a military garrison close to the Gorskis' house, our location is pinpointed for bombing attacks. With these bombings, the Nazi soldiers flee for their lives.

As the bombing begins, Irene runs to join me in the attic. She tells me that the Gorskis are leaving the house and going into the cellar, which is the laundry room in the back yard. Irene says that the couple "did not want to die with Jews in their midst," and refuse to allow us access to the cellar for protection. We guess that if they were found with Jews in their home, they would be killed for being Jew lovers.

Irene moves close to me as we crouch in the attic near the corner of the room, which makes my bed. Russian bombs fall all around our house, and their thunderous noise surrounds the attic, as everything seems to shake in our hiding place from their powerful effect. We huddle together and put our arms around each other trying to feel safe, despite the fact that the shells will most surely kill us.

A powerful explosion lifts us both into the air as part of the tin roof flies away as a bomb explodes right next to our house. My coat that was hanging on a nail in the post, which supports the roof, is suddenly ripped full of shrapnel holes. We look up and most of the roof has now been blown off the house. It is clear that we are in deadly danger, and the Russians believe the Germans are still in our little village.

With that, Irene and I look upward and see the planes continuing to fly overhead. We immediately decide to

I Still See Her Haunting Eyes

99

leave the attic and hide in safer surroundings. Thinking it would be better to be at ground level, for the first time in over two years, we both leave our hiding place and exit the house. Holding each other's hands, we run to the backyard and lie in some of the craters that have been made by the bombs. We stay there huddled together against the neighbor's fence.

As we look around, we notice that the neighbor has done the same thing and also is trying to hide in his back yard. He starts to pray loudly and crosses himself as a bullet from the strafing Russian airplane hits his head and kills him instantly. Both Irene and I scream and bury ourselves as far into the craters as possible.

When the bombing subsides, Irene and I take advantage of the situation and hide in the apartment that was deserted by the Nazi soldiers. Looking for food, we rummage through its contents. Perhaps because they fled in such a hurry, we discover bread and marmalade that was left behind, and we rejoice.

Irene and I grab pieces of the bread and the thick jelly and begin to stuff our mouths with the treasures. We prop ourselves against the wall and eat as if it was a serene day, despite the fact that bombs are falling around us. They continue, and we are jostled up in the air from the impact, but both of us refuse to let go of our bread and marmalade. For whatever reason, the bombs create no fear for us, because all we can focus on is the ability to consume massive quantities of food for the first time in two years.

When the bombing stops and all the Germans have left, the Gorskis are uncertain what to do with us. Of course the Gorskis are afraid that some of their neighbors will spy us and discover that they have been hiding Jews. They fear that the Poles will not take kindly to those who have hidden us.

We can no longer go to the attic because it is destroyed, and the only place available for us is the chicken coop. Naturally, the chickens are evicted and roam in the backyard as we occupy their abode. For four or five days we stay in the chicken coop with Irene on the lower layer and me above. We are fearful being outside and unprotected, but there is also an excitement because we are able to smell the air and look up at the stars. This is a luxury we have missed for so very long. Irene and I love being together, but we are uncertain if we will remain here undetected for long.

On the fifth day, Ukrainian soldiers begin deserting the area and start to run back to their homes. The Russians enter our town, but not before two of the Ukrainians come into the backyard. Hoping to discover food, they rip open the chicken coop door where we are hiding. Defenseless we stand there waiting to die. It is obvious to them that we are hidden Jews. One of the soldiers puts a pistol to Irene's head.

What can I do?

After two years in hiding, I'm going to die at the hands of a Ukrainian looking for food. Though petrified, I look around, but there is nowhere to hide or run. It feels like my nightmare is becoming a reality. *Please, please, I don't want to die!* I hold my breath, waiting to feel what I had feared, the pain that comes with death.

I must look down like I did in the Market Place so long ago. Maybe this will all go away …

Just at that moment, the other Ukrainian calls out to his comrade. He yells that he has found chickens and eggs, and the soldier with the gun lowers his weapon to his side and runs to his friend to gather the food.

Luck finds us. How could we be so fortunate? We have lived in hiding for almost two years, survived the bombing attack by the Russians, and spared from the bullets that killed the neighbor in the back yard. This moment we have been saved from the murderous Ukrainians.

Perhaps G-d was now listening?

Aaron Elster:
Holocaust
survivor

Chapter 15
Survivors Return
to Sokolow

A few days later, some survivors begin to show up in our town. These survivors are the lucky ones who have successfully hidden in the forest, or been liberated from work camps and concentration camps, or have lived with Russian partisans. With nothing but the clothes they wear, they enter the city that was once their home called Sokolow.

Mrs. Gorski tells us about what happened to our mother while I was living in the attic. She says that my mother and Gedala survived in hiding for most of the war. They were caught hiding in a past customer's nearby barn just three months ago.

I hold Irene's hand as Mrs. Gorski tells how three neighboring Polish men blocked the barn door so they could not escape. She says that Czeslaw Uzieblo and two neighbors wrestled my mother and Gedala to the ground and then tied them up. The gruesome story continued as she says that she actually saw them tied behind an old manure wagon and literally dragged into town.

At that point, my mother and Gedala were turned over to the Gestapo. Mrs. Gorski says she knows the Gestapo took both my mother and Gedala to the old Russian cemetery and shot them in cold blood. Mrs. Gorski quietly tells us that our mother was pregnant at the time.

My fate is sealed. My father and baby sister Sara were sent to Treblinka to die during the liquidation of Sokolow, and my mother has been exterminated only months before my return. I look down at the ground, but I have no tears. My heart feels dead, even though I breathe. There is nothing to say. We are two orphans with no living relatives. We have only each other. There is no one to find alive if we go back home.

There are two families that have survived by the names of Rafolowicz and Greenberg. Mrs. Gorski finds out about the survivors and brings Mrs. Rafolowicz to the chicken coop where we are hiding. Shocked to see Jewish survivors, Irene and I eagerly exit the hiding spot. Mrs. Rafolowicz puts her hand on my shoulder and says the few remaining survivors are gathering together in one building in town for safety.

Irene and I can hardly walk. We each weigh approximately 60 pounds and are covered in filth, vermin and lice. But … we are alive! Mrs. Rafolowicz agrees to take us, and we leave the Gorskis without ever looking back. I probably should thank them for their protection, but I walk away hoping to never again think of this place or the Gorskis.

As we walk with Mrs. Rafolowicz, I can't believe that I am finally free. I am walking down the dirt path that almost two years ago brought me to my attic prison. I might biologically be a 12-year-old, but I feel as though I am an adult who has endured a lifetime of trauma and pain.

The Rafolowicz family owned a two-story building in Sokolow prior to the war. The building, located on Dluga Street houses four apartments. Surprisingly, the house is still intact within the old ghetto area, and the decision is made that Irene and I will join the family on the top floor of the house.

Mr. and Mrs. Greenberg are also survivors who hid in the forest and occupy the apartment with the Rafolowiczs. This couple is the sister and brother-in-law of Mrs. Rafolowicz. Together we all occupy this humble dwelling.

Uncovering a mass grave in Sokolow in 1945. *(Photo courtesy United States Holocaust Memorial Museum)*

An immensely large room is divided with sheets, which are hung to separate the rooms for privacy. Still full of lice and vermin, Irene and I stay in one corner.

The town is so small. Mrs. Kucewiczowi, the restaurant owner who gave me my treasured bread when I was running away after the liquidation, comes to meet us and see if she can assist. She decides to help Irene, cleans and delouses her, and gives her new clothes. Irene is then able to work as a waitress in the restaurant for this kind and loving woman.

I basically am becoming a "street kid." Food is scarce, and all of the survivors struggle. I remain living with the Rafolowicz family, but I am forced to find my own food to survive. The family tells me that I must try to go to a different survivor's house each day to see what I can scrounge up for myself. This is a humiliating experience because food is so scarce, and I feel terrible taking anything from people who have so little. It feels demeaning to beg, and I feel like a freeloader, but I don't know how to remedy the situation. All I can do is try to find my own food, so it is one less responsibility for the Rafolowiczs.

There is a tailor (he was also a ghetto policeman) who lives with his sister in a small house. He tells me that he will give me food if I find some charcoal. The charcoal, he says, is needed to press the suits or coats for his local customers. To find this charcoal I must wander through bombed-out ruins of the town and collect the charcoal for his use.

I enter the burned-out building that used to be our house. It is now in ruins. Looking around, I feel like a stranger in this destroyed house that once held my family. This place looks nothing like a home … It looks like something foreign and desolate. Nothing of my family remains but my memories.

I begin ripping pieces of charcoal from the charred remains of the wooden walls, but nothing supports the walls, which makes this duty quite dangerous. I am joined by a little boy who keeps me company. I grab a piece of charcoal as he kicks an imaginary soccer ball. Just then, an unexploded grenade erupts and rips into his stomach. I stand there unhurt, looking at the boy's intestines, which are now outside his body. I stare at what was once my new companion. I feel sick to my stomach and have the dry heaves for hours.

As the days pass, the last of the survivors move back to town. Out of the entire Jewish population that dwelled in Sokolow, only 29 people survive from more than 5,000 Jewish inhabitants! Only two Sokolow children survived the horrors of the war on their own, my sister Irene and I.

A Jewish Russian major takes a liking to me, and I enjoy hanging around with him. The young major lets me spend time at the post, but I seem to be unable to eat the army food he offers, because I have not eaten normal food for so long. It is difficult for me to absorb and digest, and I constantly have the runs and feel sick to my stomach. How ironic it is that I am desperately starving for food, and yet my body will not accept its nourishment.

The major spends time with me, and I feel good when I'm in his presence. He says he will try to find a way to send me to Moscow and tells me stories about the beautiful city that glistened like a gem in the East. I listen intently trying to imagine the buildings he describes and try to visualize how I would look walking down the streets of Moscow. It all sounds remarkable, and I pray that he can find a way to take me with him when he returns to his homeland.

Russian is now becoming a second language I can speak conversationally. The major teaches me some Russian songs, which reminds me of songs I sang as a child with my family. Sometimes he takes me to see propaganda movies about the heroism of the partisans and the sacrifices that are made for Russia and Stalin. I enjoy

One of the remaining Jewish tomb-stones in Sokolow after the war. *(Photo courtesy Yad Vashem Film and Photo Archive)*

watching the movies and am thankful that the Russians entered our land to rid us of the demonic Nazis.

But, anti-Semitism has not faded, and the survivors are not welcomed back in Sokolow. Many of the Poles are angry that Jewish survivors insist on taking back their own property and goods. Irene told me that one of the Jewish survivors went back to a nearby farm to reclaim his land, and the current occupant hit him in the head with a sledgehammer. The man was murdered for trying to claim what was rightfully his property. Once again, the fear increases for the few Jews who have survived the Holocaust in Poland. Life after the war, in many ways, does not seem much better than before the war.

I am told that that Czeslaw Uzieblo, the man who "turned in" my mother and Gedala, will go on trial for murder. Irene and I begin to hear rumors that we must denounce the accusations of his guilt, or we will be killed. Soon Uzieblo's wife comes to us and tells us that we must testify on his behalf and sign paperwork stating that he assisted our survival by offering us food and shelter. This is all a big lie! But, what choice do we have?

The Jewish survivors tell us to sign the paperwork. The family of Czeslaw Uzieblo says if we do not protect him, there will be retribution upon us and the Jewish community. Irene and I decide to sign the documents because we are very fearful that the Poles will harm us. She signs one document, and I must sign an identical one as well.

In December 1944, the Polish Police Court sentences Uzieblo to five years in jail. He tells the court that he believes it is legal to kill Jews and that his brother had killed a Jew and nothing happened to him for this act. Uzieblo's crime is documented as being guilty of turning in a "Polish National." How strange … a Jew is not called a vile pig by the Polish Police, but called a Polish National? Czeslaw is jailed, and the other two men escape punishment, blaming everything on Czeslaw.

After that episode and the rising anti-Semitism, the majority of Sokolow Jews decide it will be safer to move from our hometown. But, to my surprise, my Uncle Sam Scherb returns to Sokolow. As he walks into town with Russian partisans, my eyes almost pop out. My mouth must have dropped to the ground. I had believed that everyone in our family had been exterminated, and now my Uncle Sam, my mother's brother, has returned to me.

I had known that he had escaped Sokolow in 1939 into the Russian-occupied zone of Poland, and then he was captured by the advancing Germans in June 1941 and

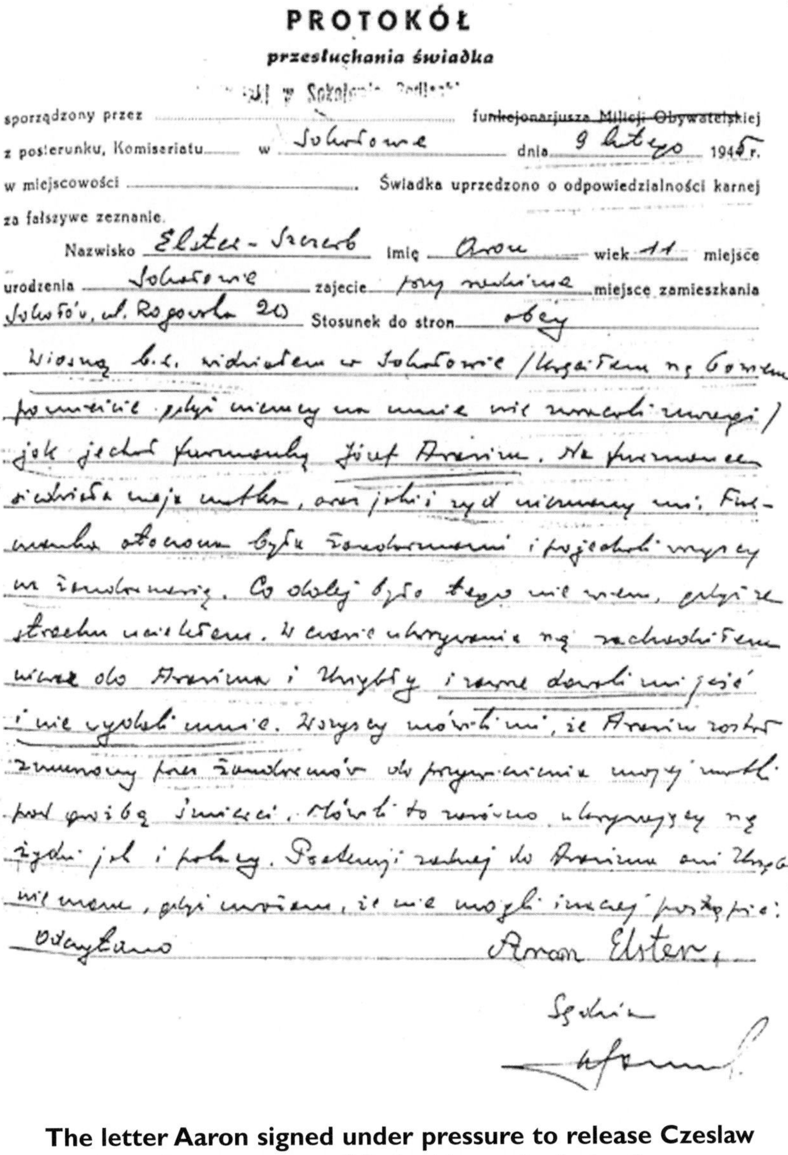

PROTOKÓŁ

przesłuchania świadka

Sąd w Sokołowie Podlaskim

sporządzony przez .... ~~funkcjonariusza Milicji Obywatelskiej~~

z posterunku, Komisariatu .... w Sokołowie dnia 9 lutego 1945 r.

w miejscowości .... Świadka uprzedzono o odpowiedzialności karnej za fałszywe zeznanie.

Nazwisko Elster-Szczerb imię Aron wiek 11 miejsce urodzenia Sokołowie zajęcie pomoc rodzinna miejsce zamieszkania Sokołów, ul. Rogowska 20 Stosunek do stron obcy

Wiosną b.r. widziałem w Sokołowie (ukrywałem się na Gonnem pomieście gdyż niemcy na mnie nie zwracali uwagi) jak jechał furmanką Józef Arasim. Na furmance siedziała moja matka, oraz jeszcze żyd nieznany mi. Furmanka otoczona była żandarmami i pojechali wszyscy do żandarmerii. Co dalej było tego nie wiem, gdyż ze strachu uciekłem. W czasie ukrywania się zachodziłem wraz do Arasima i Uzybły i razem dawali mi jeść i nie wydali mnie. Wszyscy mówili mi, że Arasim został zmuszony przez żandarmów do przywiezienia mojej matki pod groźbą śmierci. Mówili to również ukrywający się żydzi jak i polacy. Pretensji żadnej do Arasima ani Uzybły nie mam, gdyż uważam, że nie mogli inaczej postąpić.

Odczytano

Aron Elster.

Sędzia

The letter Aaron signed under pressure to release Czeslaw Uzieblo, who was responsible for his mother's death.

Irene, Uncle Sam and Aaron

placed in the Bialystok Ghetto. It was rumored that he had escaped and joined the Russian partisans and was fighting the Germans. I thought this might have been a story that was told to ease everyone's fears of his death, but here he was in Sokolow as a returning hero.

Uncle Sam arrives in a Polish Army uniform and carrying an automatic weapon strapped across his chest. He looks so handsome and very much like a hero in his military uniform. He tells me that he has been given permission by his unit commander to visit his hometown and look for his family.

Uncle Sam tells me that we must move to Lodz, where there is a larger population of surviving Jews. Uncle Sam speaks with many of the survivors, and it is decided that Irene and I will leave Sokolow with the immigrating families. It is hopeful that there is safety in numbers.

Arriving in Lodz, I am placed in an orphanage. I feel

Aaron while living in a Lodz orphanage.

happy being here where I can have a clean bed and eat wonderful food without having to beg. I am allowed to play along the mountainside, and I join some of the other kids as we enjoy getting into wooden barrels and rolling down the hill. It is joyful to be with other children who are also orphaned. I don't feel so different because there are Jewish and non-Jewish children who are in the same situation as I am.

But, life is about to change again.

געהייליקט דעם אנדענק

עלטערן: **מרדכי** און **מאשע-רחל** שטשערב

ברודער **קלמן** שטשערב

שװעסטערן: **צביה** מיט איר מאן **חיים ישראל** עלסטעד

פייגע מיט איר מאן און קינד

פייגע

קלמן

צביה

חיים ישראל

A page from the Sokolow book in memory of his family, including his grandparents names. Pictured are his aunt Feige, uncle Kalman, and his parents, Cywia and Chaim Sruel Elster. (Memorial Book of Sokolow-Podlaski)

Aaron holding a baby after the war.

I Still See Her Haunting Eyes

Chapter 16
Leaving Poland

While I'm living at the Lodz orphanage, my uncle tells me that we are going to try to escape this wretched land that has been soaked with the blood of our families.

He tells me that he is going to discover a way to leave Poland. Within a few days, he has devised his plan, and he appears in plain clothes and says he has gotten rid of his Polish uniform so that we could travel less noticeably. Uncle Sam says he has bribed a Russian soldier into smuggling us across the border into Czechoslovakia.

The journey begins and Uncle Sam, Irene and I manage to enter Czechoslovakia and stay in Prague for a few days. We have no documents, which are called "papers," and we have no money. As we try to enter Germany, we are caught by American Military Police, who send us back to Czechoslovakia. Frustrated we wonder if we will ever make our way to the American-occupied zone of Germany.

The following day we try once again, but this time my uncle has created a different plan. In the middle of the night, the three of us board a train, and when the MPs try to capture us, we exit the train on the opposite side. The three of us run, for what seems endlessly, until we reach the forest. We sleep in the forest for the rest of the night, and in the morning my uncle finds a guide who helps us escape into Germany.

After we find our way to Germany, we live in a displaced persons' (DP) camp in Fuerth (near Nuremberg), which was supported by an American organization. My uncle stays in the DP camp in Fuerth, and Irene and I are sent to a rural location so we can learn farming. We are told that a high-ranking Nazi official once owned this farm. This farm is patterned like a kibbutz, a collective farm in Palestine.

But, as we are ready to climb into the truck, the adults decide they don't want to be burdened with two children. An army chaplain hears the dispute and tells the adult members that if we are not allowed to join, they will not be transported to the farm. So, at his insistence, we all board the truck and travel to the farm. Irene and I are told that we will be transferred to Palestine after we learn the skills needed for an effective transfer.

My sister works in the kitchen, and I am told to learn farming. This is the last thing I want to learn. I remember we had a garden in our backyard in Sokolow, which brought me joy watching my father plant and reap the harvest. But farming only brings me sadness because it makes me think of my father. Who would want to be a farmer, whether it is in Germany or Palestine? I hate being the only kid on the farm, and the adults are always "pushing me" around, and I despise it. All I want to do is hang out with the American GIs, who treat me like a friend.

At 13, I am a rebel. I have a pistol that was once owned by my Uncle Sam when he was in the Polish Army. Of course, having a gun is strictly forbidden on the farm. On this farm, there are about 30 or 40 adults and just two children, Irene and me. When the governing committee discovers I have a gun, I am called to appear in front of the group for disciplinary action. The group of men scream and tell me that I am putting them all in jeopardy for having a gun. I don't care what they tell me, I will not give up the gun. I feel powerful knowing no one will ever harm me again, as long as I have this weapon.

Aaron with a friendly cow at the kibbutz.

The group becomes angrier with me, and a tall man with dark hair comes over and slaps me in the face several times. I feel the burning pain on my cheek, but I will not give up my gun that was given to me by my Uncle Sam. The discussion continues as I rub my cheek, and finally I decide to trade my gun with an American GI who is willing to exchange it for his silver harmonica. I really want to keep the gun, but it serves no real purpose. There is nothing I can do with the pistol, but I can play with this cool harmonica all the time.

I did secretly want to keep the gun in case I ever found Hitler or one of the Nazis who murdered my family. Of course, this fantasy was ridiculous because Hitler was already dead, and some of the Nazis had fled Germany at the end of the war. But, it felt wonderful to think of revenge for the death of my mother, father, and baby sister Sara and all of my aunts and uncles who perished at their hands.

The American GIs let me scout for them, and they give me cigarettes and chocolate that is wrapped in a heavy dark wax cardboard. The GIs don't know it, but I don't smoke the cigarettes or eat the candy, but instead I sell my treasures for cash to eager customers on the black market.

I accomplish this successful business venture by taking my treasures, hopping a train at night and selling my valuables at the DP camp in Neu Freimann. Playing hide and seek with the train conductor, I have mastered the art of deception and am able to journey on the train for free. After my sales in the camp, I have money in my pocket and feel powerful.

My stay at the farm is short, and I am sent back to the DP camp and allowed to stay with my uncle in Neu Freimann, which is near Munich. I enjoy being with my uncle instead of being forced to farm. I am able to go to school with regular children, which makes me feel normal. I learn to read and write Hebrew and enjoy this opportunity.

Uncle Sam and I occupy a one-room apartment on the second floor of a building in the camp. My uncle is quite popular in the camp because everyone knows he was a professional soccer player. I feel really proud to be his nephew, and there are some times that we go outside and play soccer in the campground. I feel like king of the

Going through inspection upon returning to the DP camp.

world playing soccer with my famous uncle.

But soon my uncle finds a lovely girlfriend, and I end up living in the apartment by myself for a while. I miss him, but I understand that he is eager to be in a relationship and begin his new life. Living alone is pleasant and I am happy, but I do miss my uncle's company.

A short while later, my uncle rents the other side of the room to a newlywed couple who had just moved into the camp. Even though I'm curious about sex, it's really awkward living with newlyweds, because they're always touching each other and doing "the dirty deed." But I am grateful to have a nice place to stay and have all the comforts not afforded me in the attic.

There are some wonderful benefits living in the camp. I am able to make friends with the GIs and feel special. During the day I am able to go to the public kitchen, which has a table filled with peanut butter and jelly. I love making "p and j" sandwiches. Every day I go to the table and never eat any of the other food in the commissary. I seem never to tire of the sweet and sticky combination that brings a smile to my face.

There is a woman who works for the American organization helping with the DP camp, and she really seems to like me. She thinks I am really cute and wants me to have some new clothes. She decides to make me my own military outfit. Taking a blanket, she creates a suit with pants and an "Eisenhower" jacket. I feel powerful in this outfit, and very proud. It has been a very long time since anyone has given me special attention. I cherish this outfit and make sure I am careful when I wear it.

On another day, this same woman calls me over and tells me she has another surprise for me. What could be better than the suit she made for me? She tells me to close my eyes and puts a little Kodak box camera in my hands. I can't believe I have my own camera. I promise her I will protect this camera and keep it with me always.

Aaron on the soccer field at the Displaced Persons camp at Neu Freimann.

There is a GI named Maurice who is from Boston, Massachusetts. I don't really know exactly where that is, but I know it is in America. He tells me about his hometown, and it seems like he is really interested in my sister. When we are together we do "boy things," and his GI buddies teach me to cuss in English. I learn every cuss word they teach me, but sometimes I get a slap because I don't know what the words mean and I offend someone. Either way, it's cool because I feel like I have friends who teach me neat things.

During this time we find out that we have distant relatives who live in New York. We also learn that we have some other relatives who live in a place called Chicago, which is located in the United States, too. The Chicago relatives are related to my grandfather, and one is a stepbrother to my grandpa. With that news, Irene and I are assisted by the immigration agency HIAS under something called a "children's quota" and told that we are being sent to America!

Life is about to change, once again.

The American volunteer who made Aaron a uniform and gave him a camera.

Aaron, Irene and Uncle Sam.

Aaron taking a spin on a new friend's motorcycle.

Above, Aaron, front right, at his uncle Sam Scherb's
wedding to Lili.

On the facing page, Aaron, center of middle row, at the
displaced persons camp in Neu Freimann outside of
Munich, Germany in 1947.

Images from the Neu Freimann displaced persons camp where Aaron stayed after the war before coming to America. Above, Aaron is at the right. Below, he's third from right in the back row.

Members of the soccer team that Aaron's uncle Sam coached at the displaced persons camp. Aaron is pictured in the middle kneeling in front of the visiting American GI.

Chapter 17
The Journey to America

While in the Munich DP camp, I join some other kids and we go to a "real" movie house. I have never seen a movie house. When the Russians first came to our town they placed a large movie screen outside of the Market Place and showed us movies about all the heroic things the Russians had done during the war.

But these American movies are entirely different. American movies have cowboys that have wonderful adventures. I might not understand all the words in the shoot-em-up movies, but I am able to follow the plot. I know who are the good guys and who are the bad guys, and I want to go to this place called America and meet all the good guys.

On June 7, 1947, my dream comes true. Irene and I leave Bremerhaven on a ship called the Marine Marlin and land in New York. When we pull into the harbor, we pass a huge greenish statue of a beautiful lady holding up a torch. I look at her and hope this torch of liberty would protect me from all the people that try to take away other people's freedom and rights. I hope to meet the "good guys."

When we arrive, we are taken to an orphanage. Irene and I put away our few personal items. I decide to walk alone and count the six steps that take me from the front door to the sidewalk. Right before me is a candy shop! It is an entire shop that is in the basement of this building. I decide to walk right in with my savings of two whole dollars. I must be in heaven because of all the wonderful things I see in front of my eyes. The colors within this store are more striking that anything I have ever seen. I notice a candy bar wrapped in white paper with red lettering on it. I can't read what it says, but I buy it for five cents.

As fast as I pay for the candy bar, I devour it. Then I walk a little further and see something on a stick covered with chocolate. It is something very cold made into a hardened rectangle and it tastes like milk. It is covered with chocolate, and I hold it by a little stick to eat it. I don't know what it is called, but I think it is ice cream like we had in Sokolow when I was little.

I just can't help myself; I keep seeing things that look so good. I walk from counter to counter and buy this and that, and eat everything like a crazy person. I must be eating a lot of stuff, because all of the sudden, I start to feel sick to my stomach. I don't know what to do, but I know I need to get out of the candy store, and right *now*! When I reach the sidewalk, I throw up everything I've just eaten. I lost half of my money buying candy, and for sure I am losing everything that was in my stomach!

Being in New York is like nothing I've ever imagined. I can't believe everything I am seeing. Sokolow did not have indoor plumbing or anything modern. This town has vehicles called streetcars and huge things called skyscrapers. The buildings are so tall, and I really don't understand how they stand up without falling down. Walking along all I see are lights … lights everywhere! There are so many colors that catch my eyes, and it's like a circus, and I don't know what to look at first. Everything is so amazing and different from my hometown and so full of activity.

Our stay in New York is short, and Irene and I meet some of our distant cousins who had written us when we were in Germany. They are very nice and try to help. My aunt makes me something called French fries, and I think this is one of the most wonderful treats I've ever tasted.

I Still See Her Haunting Eyes

There is a group of Sokolow survivors who live in New York, and a man named Mr. Friedman, from the "Sokolower Farein," takes us out and buys us some brand new clothes. I am excited to have some new things, but Irene seems to be elated at picking out new clothes for the upcoming trip to Chicago.

In late July 1947, we travel to Chicago to live with the Elster family on my grandfather's side. I am placed in sixth grade even though I am almost 15, which is really embarrassing. How can I fit in with kids who are five years younger than me? I feel really stupid, but I can't speak English, so I must work very hard to work up to my potential. Gradually, I am allowed to skip grades, and eventually they let me go into high school.

There is another change, because I am now going to live with a foster family. They have their own children and foster children who live in their house as well. The father is a quiet and very nice man, and the mother runs the household. She is a good-hearted woman but screams often. She is a good cook, and I love it when she makes apple strudel. Both of them treat me very well, and I stay with them for almost four years.

It's really hard to fit in, and I desperately want to make friends. It is impossible to join the "in group," but I am making some new friends even though sometimes they chuckle at my broken English.

Most of the time I gain acceptance by being the jokester. My jokes make fun of my weaknesses and shortcomings, but it is worth it to be accepted in the crowd. I realize making fun of myself is hurtful, but I want everyone to like me. I want a close friend, someone who will let me confide all the real stories of my past, but I can't seem to find anyone. Perhaps part of the problem is that I don't feel equal to the American kids, and I really can't contribute much at all ... and besides, part of me has been tarnished by my past, and I feel so insecure and damaged.

Aaron in America.

I Still See Her Haunting Eyes

Some of the kids at school think I'm arrogant, but they don't understand that I act this way because I know that basically I'm shy. They say I never smile, and I would agree, because I still have so much hurt and pain locked inside. In fact, I still have nightmares of being chased and murdered. Just before I die in my dream, I wake up totally soaked in sweat. These nightmares seem to rule my life, and sometimes I find myself unwilling to allow myself to sleep for fear that I will have to see all of the memories over and over again. I may have left Sokolow, but it has not left me. Not a day goes by that I do not see Sara's *haunting* eyes. They are in my dreams, and they follow me through the day, with each step I take. I carry the burden of her death with me and feel despair, guilt and sorrow.

I don't know what I'm going to do when I graduate from high school, but I do know that I will never allow anyone to hurt me again. I'm a survivor, and I will never be a victim of circumstances. Sokolow and the attic may have shaped my past, but it will not mold my future.

My life has always been about change, but now, I have the ability to adapt to the changes. I realize that there are no obstacles I cannot overcome; I have seen my strength and resiliency. Today I hold my future in my hands, and I will change the world on my own terms.

Irene and Aaron in America.

History, despite its wrenching pain, cannot be unlived, but if faced with courage, need not be lived again.

Maya Angelou

Part Three:
The Lessons

Chapter 18
Telling My Story

*L*ooking out into the high school auditorium, I wonder how many students really understand the horrific atrocities that occurred during the Holocaust. I stand before them pouring out my heart and wonder why I am doing this. Exposing my deepest feelings each and every time I give this talk, it is almost as if I'm there again. But today ... yes today, I was back in 1942 again, and I could feel everything as if it was happening once again.

It's hard to fathom it was more than 60 years ago, because the pain has not subsided. Look how easily I am taken back to the memories, the trauma and the pain. The triggering can be a scent, a thought that reminds me of something from the past, something I hear, or sometimes it feels like I can just taste fear ... and suddenly, against my will, I'm back there again.

I've survived, but have I healed the heartbreak, the despair, the hurt and the anger? The nightmares still come ... I still see the faces, feel the painful hunger that drives me to madness, and the pain of being alone and helpless. The haunting fears of what happened to my baby sister replay over and over in my mind ... I feel the guilt that comes from being a survivor.

Why do I open my wounds and bleed in front of these young people? Do they really care? Can they possibly understand what happened to 6 million Jewish people? How can they comprehend the slaughter of one and a half million children, including my baby sister Sara?

Will anything I say make a difference? Is it possible that my words will touch someone and urge them to become more active or speak out instead of being a bystander? Will they take a stand

and end the indifference? Would they make the sacrifices and take the actions needed to stand up to evil, prejudice and hatred?

I look at their faces and wonder if they dare to feel what I am about to say. Will they really let my words touch their emotions and create a change?

I take a deep breath, close my eyes and connect with my inner voice that tells me I must do this.

Feeling the emotional drain from "telling my story," I take another deep breath. Looking into the audience, I see there are many students with their hands raised wishing to ask me questions. Before I answer the awaiting questions, I clear my throat and say, "More than 60 years ago on this very day, I saw my

family together for the last time." Tears start to well in my eyes as I continue ...

How can I explain how an ordinary person can become a killer and torturer of innocent people? People who believe they are doing G-d's work. The same German who believes in G-d and shows love and affection to his wife and children can commit these horrible sins.

It is 60 years later, and I am still talking about the Holocaust. Why?

It is a painful fact that more survivors of the Holocaust die each year. In a short time there will be none left. Who will speak for us? Who will tell the story? I pray the answer is you! Never forget!

It is my prayer that we, as a community of humans, learn from our mistakes. The story must be told and retold to educate and inform just what can happen if we allow prejudice, bigotry and hatred to rule our lives. The story must be told to ensure that we never become bystanders while people define someone else as different or inferior, and the target of annihilation.

You are the ones who will determine the future! You are the ones who must put an end to killing one another, just because someone appears different than you or believes in a different religion or ideology. Don't fall into the trap believing that the killers were deranged people. Not so, my friends ... They were ordinary people like you and me! They had loving families, they prayed in their house of worship, and they were convinced they were doing G-d's work by exterminating the Untermenschen, "the subhuman," the Jews and anyone else the Nazis saw as a viable target for their racism and anti-Semitism.

It is your responsibility to stand up to intolerance. You must decide if our Universe will be one of inclusion or exclusion. Compassion and dedication to creating a better world is within your grasp if you are willing to facilitate this outcome. It will not happen without work. As the Dalai Lama said, "It is not enough to be compassionate. You must also act."

I Still See Her Haunting Eyes

Be silent, and hate will flourish. Speak out, and hatred dies, because words are powerful. We all can say such horrible things to each other, or we can use our words to motivate, to encourage, to show love and to stand strong. You must use your words to be pro-active and speak out when anyone is dehumanized, regardless of race, religion or color of skin. If you don't, can you be the next victim to be persecuted? If you stand by and listen, does your apathy mean you agree? Many did not speak out when Hitler and the Nazis were spreading their hateful propaganda, and you see what happened. Doing nothing at all is being part of the problem.

Remember that hatred can be infectious. It is easy to hate, but much harder to love. You have to open your heart, and be willing to see the good in people. You have to be willing to see the Light inside the other person, and the Light in yourself. All I can see is that you are much smarter, and much tougher than you imagine.

You must guard your freedom and your right to individuality. Do not sit back and become victims; instead, you must advocate for yourself. You have to fight for what you believe, and be willing to lose it all to gain your goal. I'm not talking about money or wealth ... I'm talking about being willing to stand up to your friends or family for what you believe right and just. If you don't stand up, ignorant people will try to keep you locked in pain and suffering. You need to find your power, touch your resiliency and fight for a meaningful life. Please do not waste the chance you have been given. I fought every day to live, because I wanted it so much.

One person can make a difference. Look at the power of Gandhi, Martin Luther King, or Elie Wiesel and Oprah Winfrey. Each of us has a gift, a purpose to pursue and fulfill. Will you take the risk and pursue your purpose? Will you endure and presevere to become your ultimate self? You must believe in yourself, because you are the creator of your destiny. Fulfill your promise.

Don't underestimate the power and strength you possess. You can accomplish great things. I believe this with all my heart. I could never imagine that a young boy of 10 could have survived and done so much because he wanted to live. Nothing is impossible, not if you want it badly enough.

I ask you to search for ways to change your world for the good. Standing here today, I challenge you to never turn away ... to open your heart to new people and new ideas. Never allow yourself to become apathetic. It only leads to inhumanity and the evils that we have seen in our world.

But most of all, I ask that you take a moment and realize what is important to you. Close your eyes and think for a moment ... what is the most important thing you possess? Is it a possession like your car? Your computer? What is it?

I know the answer ... it is those you love. I'm sure of that because I lost my family on this very day 64 years ago. Nothing in the world compares to losing those you love.

When life is done with me, I want to know that I have touched this world in a positive way. There are very few things I can leave behind, but the one thing I can give is to touch people with my love, my heart and my lessons.

I love you all.

Aaron Elster

Questions and Answers:

Do you know what happened to the Gorskis?

They had difficulty trying to reestablish a life, and they were always poor. I think about them often and pray for their souls. One of my regrets in life is that I never was able to help them. I would have liked to repay them for their sacrifice. Irene sent them packages and some money, but living in a foster home made it impossible for me to do the same.

As a child I had no warm feelings about them because of the way they treated me. But now I see the enormity of the risk they took. They did make a supreme sacrifice, and they were constantly in mortal danger. I have visited their graves in Poland.

Is Irene still alive?

Yes, my sister lives in the suburbs of Chicago, and I'm so thankful for that gift from G-d. She has two married daughters and four grandchildren who make her very proud.

She and I rarely talk about the events during those years, and in some ways we have different realities, because we did have oppositional lives for those two years. The interesting thing is she is two or three years older than me, but something happened ... now when

Irene in the 1990s.

she tells the story, I am her older brother. She is a wonderful support, and I love her deeply.

Do you still think about Sara?

Each and every day. I wonder who was there to hold her little hand and assure her that all would be well? She was only six, and I have nightmares of how she was amid strangers and no one was there to help her. My tortured thoughts see her on the "death trip" and the poisonous gas that entered the gas chamber that painfully choked her life away. My heart aches for poor Sara, and it never goes away.

That is why it is so important that I speak about her … because each time I mention her name, and speak her name sweetly, she still lives, and in my heart she is always six. The Nazis could only take away her physical body, but they could not take away her memory, which is safe inside me … and now safe inside you!

What did you do in Chicago as an adult?

After high school, I worked at a shoe store called O'Connor and Goldberg. They were wonderful to me and the general manager was sort of a father fig-

Aaron as a teenager in the United States.

Serving in the United States military during the Korean War.

ure, but it was a dead-end job, with very little prospect for a bright future. After high school I was inducted into the U.S. Army and served in Korea. I was married after the war and concerned with supporting my family. I interviewed with Metlife, and I succeeded beyond my expectations, despite my fears of failure. I became a leading agent.

Suddenly, I was invited to speak at conventions and try to motivate others to follow my lead. I'd speak about my start with the company, my success, and I was considered an "inspirational speaker." I would say these things, but somehow I didn't feel any of it was real. It feels like it was just a fluke.

In 1993, I decided to retire, and I've been involved with the Holocaust Memorial Foundation for all those years. I generally speak two to three times a week, and now they are sending me out to speak all over G-d's creation! I try to get into your heart, into your mind and into your soul ... and the responses from students just melt my heart. You are so powerful ... you have such big hearts. I have such a respect for youngsters.

Do you think your past contributed to your success as an adult?

Of course. The fear of death and my fear of failure have been my greatest motivators. In my business life, the will to work and achieve drives me to reach my goals. All else was chance. I am no smarter, or no better than anyone else ... perhaps I just work hard.

Have you gone back to Poland?

Yes, I have returned to Sokolow on three occasions. In the 1980s, and twice in the 1990s. When I returned, I looked for items, documents, or papers related to my family, but there was nothing to be found. I returned to see the Gorskis' house and went into the attic. It is inter-

Aaron returned to his hometown, Sokolow, Poland in the
1980s and 1990s. Above, with the welcoming sign. Below,
the apartment he lived in with a couple of families immediately after he left the Gorskis.

The Gorskis' house still stands, above, though with a new roof. Below, the Gorskis' tombstone.

Aaron at an old memorial in Sokolow, Poland, that once had a sign posted, "No Jews or dogs allowed."

esting that the space is so tiny. When I was 12, it felt so much larger. Of course, due to the bombing during the liberation, it was necessary to put on a new roof.

There is a park where all the Jews were buried in a mass grave, and I've visited the Gorskis' grave and paid my respects to their souls for what they did for Irene and me. I will not go back there again ... there is nothing there for me.

Your mother left you. How do you feel about that?

I have to believe that she knew that I could not survive with her and Gedala. She loved me and wanted me to live, and I believe that is why she sent me to the Gorskis. She hoped that their connection (between Mrs. Gorski and my mother) was strong enough that they would be willing to hide me, as they did Irene.

It would be easy to think differently about my mother, and that perhaps she chose this German man over me. But she was my mother, and she loved me. She wanted me to live, and the only way that would be possible was for me to be in safety and hiding.

Did you ever think of turning yourself in to the authorities?

Never. Never once. When the ghetto was liquidated, the man who let me stay in his barn suggested I turn myself in. He said, "There is no hope for people like you." But, I wanted to live so desperately. The will to live is so great. I vowed I would never submit. It really speaks to how strong we are as human beings, and how important it is to believe in yourself and your ability to endure the twists and turns that life brings to each of us. Friedrich Nietzsche says, "What does not kill me makes me stronger."

Do you have anger towards Germans?

If you had asked me this question when I was 15, my answer would be totally different. At that time, my goal was to wipe Germany off the face of the earth. I wanted revenge on the Nazis for the atrocities they committed. Now, I'm an old man, and I have resolved my anger.

Hate destroys you instead of those who did the damage to you. So the result is that you are destroying your own life with the hate that burns inside. A wise man said that anger is like a hot burning coal … when you pick it up to throw it at someone, it only burns you. I know most of the murderers are dead now, and I no longer hate or have anger. But, I will not forgive. They must ask my baby sister Sara for forgiveness, not me.

Do you still have nightmares?

Yes. But the nightmares are not as often as when I was a child or a teenager. They always center on being killed, tested, horrible scenes from the past, or seeing my baby sister being taken away. Sometimes I have nightmares about being inferior, not being able to care for myself, and mostly about failure. More than anything, my adult dreams center around fear of failure. But, in my waking hours, I know that I have made peace with my fears, and realize that the only thing that can hurt me now is to not allow myself to live a purposeful, loving life.

How did you meet your wife?

They say all's fair in love and war. As a teen, I met my wife at a party when she was on a date with my friend. What can I say? I liked what I saw, and Jackie and I have been together ever since. We've been married for more than 50 years. She was the first one who ever said she loved me, and that was at the age of 21.

Have you come back to your faith?

Yes. I have battled with it most of my life. I cannot conceive a G-d that would allow the slaughter of little children, and stand by watching. In spite of it all, I have made my peace with G-d. It is hard to believe certain things, but I have been told not to question … but I am an old man, and anyway, soon I will find out for myself if G-d exists.

Jackie and Aaron as newlyweds.

152

Would you have been willing to die so Sara could live?

This is a difficult question. No one knows what he or she would be willing to do in the face of death. I can't answer that question with total truth in my heart. But, I know that each and every day Sara lives through me. And rhetorically speaking, a part of me did die with Sara during those years.

Could this happen again?

Look around you … it is happening right now. Hate still fills our world. People are still killing because of differences, because of skin color. What have we learned? People are always looking for someone to blame.

After World War I, the Germans had endured a devastating blow financially, and they needed someone to use as a scapegoat. It was the Jews. But, look around … you can be the next scapegoat. That is why you must make the change in your world, and I believe you have the power to make the change.

Aaron returns to the Market Place in Sokolow where he last saw his father and sister Sara.

About the authors
Aaron Elster

Aaron Elster is a child survivor of the Holocaust. He was born in 1932 in the small village of Sokolow in northeastern Poland. Aaron lived in the Sokolow Ghetto with his two sisters, mother and father until the liquidation of the ghetto in 1942.

He escaped the liquidation and hid in various surrounding farms. Eventually, Aaron found refuge in the attic of a Polish family, where he hid for two years until the war's end. After the war, he lived in several orphanages throughout Poland, and eventually was smuggled out of Poland to various DP camps in West Germany.

Aaron Elster and his sister Irene came to the United States in June 1947. He was educated in Chicago and served in the armed forces in Korea. Aaron has been married to his wife Jackie for more than 50 years. They have two sons, Robert and Steven, and two grandchildren, Allison and Sarah.

Aaron worked for Metlife for almost 40 years. He was a leading sales representative, including 17 years as a manager. He was inducted into the Metlife Hall of Fame.

I Still See Her Haunting Eyes

After retirement, he became an active member of the community, serving as co-chairman of the Speakers Bureau and Vice President of the Executive Board at the Holocaust Memorial Foundation of Illinois. His presentations touch adults and children alike, and his open and loving style creates extensive discussions and interactive exploration of the Holocaust and its issues. Within his presentation, Aaron challenges young people to explore their strengths and encourages them to be the master of their destiny, realizing that they have the power to change their world.

When he is not teaching about the Holocaust, Aaron enjoys playing golf, spending time with his family, and telling some good jokes and kibitzing.

You can contact Aaron Elster with your questions or for a speaking engagement by contacting The Illinois Holocaust Memorial Foundation of Illinois/Illinois Holocaust Museum and Educational Center at at *www.hmfi.org.*

Joy Erlichman Miller, Ph.D., LCPC

Joy Erlichman Miller, Ph.D., is an internationally known licensed psychotherapist, professional trainer and author. Miller is the founder and director of Joy Miller & Associates in Peoria, Illinois. Dr. Miller is an Illinois state Licensed Clinical Professional Counselor as well as a Certified Master Addictions Counselor. Additionally Dr. Miller has been a part-time instructor at Bradley University and was a faculty member at Walden University in the doctoral psychology program.

A frequent expert on national syndicated television, Dr. Miller has appeared on the Sally Jessy Raphael, Oprah Winfrey, Jenny Jones, Montel Williams and Geraldo Rivera shows. Dr. Miller hosted her own radio show for five years on a CBS affiliate radio station and currently presents a weekly mental health segment on the local CBS television station. Miller was also a columnist for a Peoria area newspaper, writing a weekly mental health column.

In 1996, Dr. Miller was presented with the Harold Hodgkinson Dissertation Award for her doctoral dissertation entitled, *The Coping Strategies and Adaptation Mechanisms Utilized by Female Holocaust Survivors from the*

I Still See Her Haunting Eyes

Auschwitz Concentration Camp. Dr. Miller has also been the recipient of the Harold Baer Award and the Outstanding Alumni Award from Bradley University, as well as the Peg Burke Award from the Mental Health Association of Illinois Valley, and numerous other community awards.

Miller is the author of six published books, which include, *Following the Yellow Brick Road: The Adult Child's Personal Journey Through Oz; My Holding You Up is Holding Me Back: Over-Responsibility and Shame; Celebrations for Your Inner Child; Addictive Relationships: Reclaiming Your Boundaries;* and *Love Carried Me Home: Women Surviving Auschwitz,* which is an in-depth look at the resilient struggle of 16 women during the Holocaust. All proceeds from the work are donated to the United States Holocaust Memorial Museum. Her latest publication is called *Cancer: Here's How YOU Can Help ME Cope and Survive.*

Currently, Dr. Miller is active in numerous projects focused at ending prejudice, intolerance and hatred in our country, including chairing the Peoria Holocaust Memorial, which created a glass memorial filled with 11 million buttons to honor each of the victims of the Holocaust.

Dr. Miller has served on numerous central Illinois boards of directors, including the Mental Health Association, the Junior League, The Center for the Prevention of Abuse, Women's Health Network, Methodist Medical Center, Peoria Area Red Cross, and Children's Hospital of Illinois. Miller was named to the national advisory board of the American Red Cross Holocaust and War Victims Tracing Center in Baltimore, MD. She was the co-founder of Peoria's Teen Crisis Line. She is also one of the organizers and founders of the Women's Lifestyle Show, which celebrates the power of women.

Photograph credits

**Memorial Book of Sokolow-Podlaski; edited by
M. Gelbart. Printed in Tel Aviv, by the landsmanshaften from Israel and America in 1962.**
Landsmanshaften *means former residents. Though each
photo has been clearly marked with the resource, numerous
unsuccessful attempts were made to locate representatives
of the above volume. If any are found, please contact BF
Press for inclusion in future printings.*

**The United States Holocaust Memorial Museum,
Washington, D.C.**
*The views or opinions expressed in this book, and the content
in which the images are used, do not necessarily reflect the
views or policy of, nor imply approval or endorsement by, the
United States Holocaust Memorial Museum.*

**Yad Vashem Photo and Film Archive, The
Holocaust Martyrs' and Heroes' Remembrance
Authority, Jerusalem, Israel**

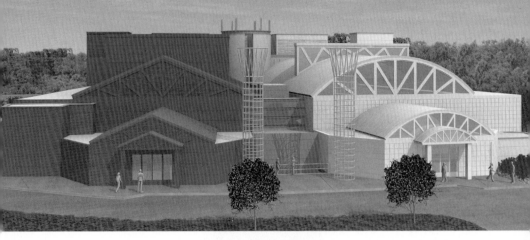

Invitation

It is stories such as Aaron Elster's that will be conveyed in the new Illinois Holocaust Museum and Education Center, now under construction in Skokie.

This 65,000 square-foot facility will reach students, teachers, parents and children throughout Illinois and across the Midwest, educating them about this tragic period in history and alerting them to the dangers of unchallenged bigotry. A project of the Holocaust Memorial Foundation of Illinois, the new museum will help visitors apply the lessons of the Holocaust to issues of hate, bigotry, and intolerance in our world today. The museum will become a cherished destination for learning and reflection, as well as an instrument for strengthening inter-ethnic understanding throughout our region. We hope you will join with us as this magnificent project comes to life. For more information on the new museum, please visit http://www.hmfi.org

Richard S. Hirschhaut
Project and Executive Director
Illinois Holocaust Museum and Education Center